KING PROSPERITY

GOD'S PLAN
FOR SUCCESSFUL
FINANCIAL STEWARDSHIP

RUSSELL GROSS

PurposeQuest Ink
P.O. Box 8882
Pittsburgh, PA 15221-0882
412.646.2780

Table of Contents

Dedication and Acknowledgments   v

Introduction   vii

Part I – Foundational Principles
    Chapter 1 – Should We Or Shouldn't We?   3
    Chapter 2 – What God Has To Say About Money   11
    Chapter 3 – What God Has To say About Debt   23

Part II – Achieving Kingdom Prosperity
    Chapter 4 – Tithes & Offerings: God's Financial Plan   37
    Chapter 5 – Presenting the Tithes & Offerings to the Lord: How   57
        We Give Matters

Part III – The Principles Of Stewardship
    Chapter 6 – Stewardship 101: Taking care of God's stuff God's way   77
    Chapter 7 – Stewardship 102: What are your financial priorities?   91
    Chapter 8 – Stewardship 103: Your Budget – Roadmap to   103
        Successful Financial Stewardship
    Chapter 9 – Stewardship 104: Self-Discipline and Faith –   131
        The way to stay on track

Part IV – Conclusion
    Chapter 10 – Practical Principles for Kingdom Prosperity: 147
        Mixing Common Sense with Biblical Wisdom
    Chapter 11 – The Challenge: What are you going to do now?   159

Endnotes   163

Dedication and Acknowledgements

This book is dedicated to my late wife Beverly, who went to be with the Lord on October 25, 2007. She was truly a woman of God, and the woman God always intended me to have. She was my wife for more than 28 years, and my best friend, lover, confidant, advisor, and most of all, my partner for life. She inspired me to develop and teach the courses which this book is based upon, and worked with me to make them a reality. She would teach the sections of the course that addressed negotiating with creditors, because when that was necessary in our home, she was the one who did that. She had the patience and right disposition to do it, which I didn't always have. But that's what a partnership is all about: sharing, supporting and building upon each other's strengths and weaknesses. To the love of my life, forever missed, always with me and never forgotten, this book is for you!

I would be remiss if I didn't recognize God, my Creator, Deliverer, Strength, Source, Rock, my Salvation, Sanctifier, Righteousness, heavenly Father, my everything, the One through whom all things are possible, and who imparted His revelation and wisdom on financial stewardship to me. God is the real author of this book, the One who without this book truly could not have been written. I am just the channel to deliver it using the gifting he has given me.

There are also many men and women of God to whom I owe a debt to for this book being written. Some inspired me, some encouraged me, some supported me, some corrected me, some taught me, some I know quite well, and some I've never even met. I especially want to acknowledge the teachings of my pastor, overseer and spiritual father, Rev. Dr. Jeffery Allen Williams; the teachings of Apostle Frederick K. C. Price, John Avanzini and Mike Murdock; Dr. John Stanko, the "Purpose Doctor"; and all of the other men and women God has used to speak to me about Kingdom Prosperity and Financial Stewardship, for which I am forever grateful. I also want to thank Dr. Stanko for helping me to get this work published.

Finally, I need to thank all of my dear friends who encouraged and supported me through the years and in the writing of this book, especially my brothers and sisters in the Body of Christ and in particular at my home church the King's Cathedral. I couldn't have done this without you.

Introduction

I wrote this book out of obedience to share with others what God has revealed to me over the years regarding Kingdom prosperity and successful financial stewardship. I wish I could take credit for this material being original, but I cannot. God revealed it all to me, some through the Scriptures, some through the Holy Spirit, some through men and women of God (and some not of God), and some through all of the mistakes I made before I came to the realization that the only way to be truly successful in financial matters is doing them God's way.

I started sharing what God revealed to me by teaching courses at my local church using titles such as "God's Financial Plan", "Successful Financial Stewardship" and a few others I can't even remember now. Each one focused on being an effective steward over the financial resources with which God has blessed each of us. Next, I attempted to incorporate, albeit unsuccessfully, what God had revealed to me into a course for the prison ministry I was involved in through my local church. The program we were teaching was comprised of several different courses that each ran 10-12 weeks and were intended (and effectively did) provide life-building skills to men and women during their time of incarceration. The financial course, however, utilized a different format than the others, wasn't as well written and didn't seem to be an effective tool to train men and women about financial matters. The person in charge of the program knew I had taught financial courses at my local church and asked me to look at the book used for their course. I did and agreed to attempt to re-write the course, incorporating some material from the course I taught at my local church.

Sometimes the Lord lets you go down a certain road so you can come to the realization for yourself that that road is not the way He wants you to go. Such was the case with my attempt to rewrite the prison ministry course. Eventually I put that effort aside. Two years later, I had a burning desire to do something with the wisdom God shared with me in the area of kingdom prosperity and financial stewardship. After much prayer, fasting and consultation with people God sent to speak into my life, I knew the road God wanted to me to take to share what I had learned was to write this book. I pray this effort will be as much of a blessing and help to everyone who reads it as it was when God gave me the revelation contained therein.

I questioned if I could even write this book, something I had never done before. Who am I to do this? I am really no different than anyone else. I do not have years of professional financial expertise, haven't made what the world would say is a "killing" in the financial markets, am not financially independent, and do not have an endless source of money at my disposal. I do have a college education, had a successful business career, was married (widowed several years ago), remarried and divorced, have a son, own my home and am active in my local church, but so are many others as well.

I am also a child of God who while not being "rich" has had every financial need met since yielding to the will of God and starting to manage the financial resources He blessed me according to His way and not mine. Does that alone qualify me to write this book? I don't know the answer to that question, but what I do know is that God has called me to share what He revealed to me. He's also gifted me to teach and write. Whether or not this work sells a lot of copies is not what's important. What is important is my being obedient to the Lord while using the gifts He's blessed me with, and being a vessel through which God can touch the lives of others!

You may ask what is so special about this book, since there have been many other books on biblical prosperity and financial stewardship written by well-known authors and theologians who have had a countless number of works on this topic published. Probably nothing, but if God has directed me to write it, there must be something in it He wants to reach and teach other people, maybe even you! What this book is intended to do is help people become obedient and successful stewards of the financial blessings God has bestowed upon them, no matter how large or small they might be. It will not in and of itself make you rich or even debt free. If you apply the principles taught, however, you can equip yourself to more effectively manage what you already have and receive the greater blessing God wants you to have. That is what I pray will make this book special for you.

This book is biblically-based, but also provides practical principles and tools to help you establish and live by effective principles of financial stewardship, along with an understanding of how God expects you to use the blessings He gives you so He can give you even more. The principles provided are simple to understand and the tools easy to use. What may be difficult is making the choice to apply what you learn and to stick with it, not going back to how you've managed your financial resources in the past. That is why you are financially where you are now.

There are some basics you need to understand and keep in mind as you go through this book that are summed up in the following scriptures:

1. "So then faith comes by hearing, and hearing by the word of God" (Romans 10:17).

   We learn by repetition, continually hearing and practicing things over and over. In order to get the most out of this book, you will need to be open to the content even if you may have heard all or some of it before. By doing so, you will catch a fresh revelation of God's plan for you to prosper, and understand what that means.

2. "While we do not look at the things which are seen, but at the things which are not seen. For the things which are seen are temporary, but the things which are not seen are eternal" (2 Corinthians 4:18) and "For we walk by faith, not by sight" (2 Corinthians 5:7).

If you keep focused on the Word of God and not your circumstances, your circumstances can and will change. Yes, if you're broke, can't pay your bills and you never seem to have enough money, those are the facts and they are real. But those facts, the things seen all around you, are not the ultimate truth. The truth is the word of God, the things not seen, which can change the things seen, *if* you allow the word of God to determine how you live your life instead of your circumstances. That is walking by faith and not by sight. I encourage you to put your trust in and try God's way so you can change your financial situation. Your way, my way, any worldly way may give you some temporary success, but in the end they will all fail. God's way never fails, and your situation can change quickly.

3. "If My people who are called by My name will humble

themselves, and pray and seek My face, and turn from their wicked ways, then I will hear from heaven, and will forgive their sin and heal their land" (2 Chronicles 7:14).

In a sense God is pleading with you to stop trying to do things you way, and turn to Him, realizing who He is, and that you can never be all He intends you to be without His help. You need to humble yourself before God and submit to His will. If you try God's way, He promises to heal and forgive you, and put you in a position to be restored to the place He intended you to be before the enemy stole all you had in every area of your life, including your finances.

4. "I beseech you therefore, brethren, by the mercies of God, that you present your bodies a living sacrifice, holy, acceptable to God, which is your reasonable service. [2] And do not be conformed to this world, but be transformed by the renewing of your mind, that you may prove what is that good and acceptable and perfect will of God. [3] For I say, through the grace given to me, to everyone who is among you, not to think of himself more highly than he ought to think, but to think soberly, as God has dealt to each one a measure of faith. [4] For as we have many members in one body, but all the members do not have the same function, so we, being many, are one body in Christ, and individually members of one another. Having then gifts differing according to the grace that is given to us, let us use them: if prophecy, let us prophesy in proportion to our faith; or ministry, let us use it in our ministering; he who teaches, in teaching; he who exhorts, in exhortation; he who gives, with liberality; he who leads, with diligence; he who shows mercy,

with cheerfulness. Behave Like a Christian. Let love be without hypocrisy. Abhor what is evil. Cling to what is good. Be kindly affectionate to one another with brotherly love, in honor giving preference to one another; not lagging in diligence, fervent in spirit, serving the Lord; rejoicing in hope, patient in tribulation, continuing steadfastly in prayer; distributing to the needs of the saints, given to hospitality. Bless those who persecute you; bless and do not curse. Rejoice with those who rejoice, and weep with those who weep. Be of the same mind toward one another. Do not set your mind on high things, but associate with the humble. Do not be wise in your own opinion. Repay no one evil for evil. Have regard for good things in the sight of all men. If it is possible, as much as depends on you, live peaceably with all men. Beloved, do not avenge yourselves, but rather give place to wrath; for it is written, "Vengeance is Mine, I will repay," says the Lord. Therefore "If your enemy is hungry, feed him; If he is thirsty, give him a drink; for in so doing you will heap coals of fire on his head. Do not be overcome by evil, but overcome evil with good" (Romans 12:1-21).

I know that last one was a long passage, but I believe it is important to share these passages as they speak to attitude, having a right heart with God, and behaving like a Christian. If the principles in this book are going to be effective in your life, you need to be right before God. Yes, you are made right before God through Jesus Christ, but you are also commanded to live a Holy life. That doesn't mean being perfect, because you are not, only Jesus was. But it does mean to try and live a holy life. When you stumble and fall, which will happen from time to time, you don't stay down on yourself. You don't think you're not worthy to continue to walk in the things of God, because through Jesus you are. So ask God to forgive you and cleanse you according to His word in 1 John 1:9, and get back up and continue to follow God.

Romans 12:3 also states that everybody has the same amount of faith. It's what you do with that faith, however, that makes a difference. If you develop and use your faith, God will work in your life. It you don't, He won't. Therefore I encourage you to take what you learn from this book and exercise your faith to do it. Believe what you receive, confess it over your life, and act on it to get the best results and change your financial situation.

Also remember that it took you some time to get into your present financial situation, so it will take some time to turn it around. Don't give up if at first your financial situation seems to worsen when you begin to apply the principles and tools in this book. That's just the enemy trying to discourage you and God testing you to see if you are serious. Stay with it, and I promise that you will see your financial situation improve.

Before you move on to the Chapter One, I encourage you to review the verses above one more time. Read them from your own Bible, and ask God to open them up to you and give you the insight He has for you, which may be different than the revelation He gave me or will give others. I also suggest before you move on to Chapter One that you read the following verses and reflect on and answer the associated questions:

1. **Genesis 12:1-3**: Why do you think God wanted Abram to leave his homeland and family before he would bless him?

2. **Genesis 13:1-5**: What do you think is the significance of what God reveals to us about Abram in verses 2 and 5?

3. **Genesis 17:6**: What does "exceedingly fruitful" connote to you? Who do you the think the "kings" are that God says will come out of Abraham?

4. **Genesis 24:35:** What does this confirm about Abraham?

5. **Galatians 3:5-9; 16-18; 29:** Who do you think "those who are of the faith" are? What do you think being blessed with believing Abraham means for us today? Who is the Seed to whom the blessings of Abraham were promised? How and through whom do the blessings promised to Abraham get passed on to us?

6. **3 John 2:** What do you take this verse to mean?

7. **Hebrews 13:8:** How does this verse help to reinforce your faith that God's Word is still in force today?

8. **Romans 10:9-10:** Do you believe what these two verses say?

Part 1
Foundational Principles

God wants you to prosper.

Chapter 1

Should You or Shouldn't You?

One of the first questions you need to address before you dive into talking about Kingdom prosperity and successful financial stewardship is whether or not believers like you should prosper financially. The short answer is "Yes!" God wants you to prosper and have more than enough! If you can't first get this question settled in your heart, you will never have very much, and won't be too good at managing or keeping what you do have. This is one of the reasons many believers struggle with finances and other areas of their lives, because they've been brainwashed with religious tradition that "good Christians" like you are not supposed to have very much.

To start, let's see what God has to say about this. In Genesis 12:1-3 God told Abram (later renamed Abraham) that if he left his family and country and went to live where God would show him, God would do three things: 1) make Abram and Abram's name great; 2) bless him so he could be a blessing to others; and 3) bless all the other families of the earth through Abram. God added that he would bless those who blessed Abram and curse those who cursed Abram. I don't know about you, but this sure sounds to me like God wanted Abram to prosper, which the dictionary defines as "succeeding in enterprise or activity," "achieving economic success," "becoming strong and flourishing" and "succeeding or thriving." While being prosperous goes far beyond money, it does seem to include money.

Lest you think I am stretching the definition of being prosperous and what God said in Genesis 12:1-3, look what it says in Genesis 13 after Abram left his family and homeland along with his nephew Lot: "Then Abram went up from Egypt, he and his wife and all that he had, and Lot with him, to the South. Abram was very rich in livestock, in silver, and in gold." It's clear that Abram was loaded with an abundance of material things, which seems to fit the definition above of what it means to be prosperous. In fact, Genesis 12:5 tells you that when Abram and Lot got to the land God had shown him, it was not big enough to support all that Abram and Lot had. I hope you agree with me that Abram was very prosperous. In Genesis 17:6, God tells Abram (after God had changed his name to Abraham), "I will make you exceedingly fruitful; and I will make nations of you, and kings shall come from you." Exceedingly fruitful, make many nations of you, and kings shall come from you – that all sound like forms of prosperity to me.

If you are still not convinced that Abram, now called Abraham, was prosperous in many ways including material things, take a look at Genesis 24 where Abraham sent his servant out to find a wife for his son Isaac. I would encourage you to read the entire chapter, but for now let's focus on verse 35. After Abraham's servant had made it to Abraham's homeland and had found the young woman who would marry Isaac among Abrahams' relatives, he told the woman's father, "The Lord has blessed my master greatly, and he has become great; and He has given him flocks and herds, silver and gold, male and female servants, and camels and donkeys."

Not only do we see that it was the Lord God Himself who blessed Abraham, but the servant leaves no doubt that God blessed Abraham with flocks and herds, silver and gold, male and female servants, and camels and donkeys, none of which are spiritual, but rather natural, material possessions, including the financial possessions of silver and gold. Like I said earlier, Abraham was loaded!

I think we have established that Abraham was prosperous financially with an abundance of material possessions. You may be thinking, "Well, that's all well and good for Abraham, but what does that have to do with me today? Does it mean that God wants to prosper me like He did Abraham with material possessions like money?" Those are good questions! The answer is that the blessings of Abraham, the prosperity he had has everything to do with God wanting you to be prosperous today. Where do I get that from, you may ask, especially since Abraham was blessed under the old covenant and we are under the new covenant through Jesus? The answer can be found in the new covenant itself as explained in Galatians chapter 3:5-9:

> "Therefore He who supplies the Spirit to you and works miracles among you, does He do it by the works of the law, or by the hearing of faith? just as Abraham "believed God, and it was accounted to him for righteousness." Therefore know that only those who are of faith are sons of Abraham. And the Scripture, foreseeing that God would justify the Gentiles by faith, preached the gospel to Abraham beforehand, saying, "In you all the nations shall be blessed." So then those who are of faith are blessed with believing Abraham."

This is really interesting! God is telling you through the Apostle Paul that if you have faith you are blessed along with believing Abraham. But "of faith" about what? Verse 8 tells you that it's the gospel or good news. If you by faith have received the gospel (and I trust you have), which is what

Jesus did for us through His crucifixion, death, resurrection and ascension, then you are blessed along with Abraham. In other words, the blessings of Abraham are for every believer today, right now! Let's not stop there.

Look a bit further in Galatians 3 it gets even better. Verses 16-18 state, "Now to Abraham and his Seed were the promises made. He does not say, "And to seeds," as of many, but as of one, "And to your Seed" who is Christ. And this I say, that the law, which was four hundred and thirty years later, cannot annul the covenant that was confirmed before by God in Christ, that it should make the promise of no effect. For if the inheritance is of the law, it is no longer of promise; but God gave it to Abraham by promise."

It appears then that the promises God made to Abraham back in Genesis 12 under the old covenant, which we have seen included financial prosperity, also belong to Abraham's seed, Christ Jesus. And the icing on the cake is in Galatians 3:29: "And if you are Christ's, then you are Abraham's seed, and heirs according to the promise." Do you see what this says? If you are in Christ, in other words if you have received the free gift of salvation by faith as a result of the redemptive work Jesus did on the cross, if you have been born-again or saved and adopted into the body of Christ, then you are an heir to all of the blessings of Abraham which were passed on to His seed, Christ, and that includes prosperity, both financial and otherwise.

There you have it. It's quite clear that God wants His believing children, Believers in Christ to prosper. You need to settle this in your heart once and for all. God wants you to prosper! Even though the passages I just quoted were penned almost 2,000 years ago, if God said it then it still holds true today since according to Hebrews 13:8, God never changes: "Jesus Christ is the same yesterday, today, and forever."

How you become prosperous and how to be a good steward over the prosperity God gives you is what the rest of this book is all about. For now, get it in your mind and heart that God wants you to prosper! And if you still have doubts about God wanting you to prosper, consider more new covenant or New Testament evidence that is so simple and plain you can't miss it. It's found in 3 John 2: "Beloved, I pray that you may prosper in all things and be in health, just as your soul prospers" The phrase "in all things" includes financial prosperity as well as prosperity in every other area of your life, such as your money, marriage, children, health, job - every single area of your life. God wants His children to be prosperous!

What if you are not God's child? What if you have not received the free gift of salvation? Does this mean you cannot be prosperous? According to the Bible that we have covered in this chapter the answer would be "No!" You cannot be prosperous the way God wants you to be. The good news is that it's not too late for you to receive the free gift of salvation, become a part of the body of Christ and be one of God's children so you can position yourself to become prosperous.

How do we receive what Jesus did for us on the cross? One way is as the Apostle Paul tells us quite clearly in Romans 10:9-10: "That if you confess with your mouth the Lord Jesus and believe in your heart that God has raised Him from the dead, you will be saved. For with the heart one believes unto righteousness, and with the mouth confession is made unto salvation." It's that simple, you just need to believe this in your heart and confess it with your mouth by faith. If you've never done that before, I encourage you to seriously consider doing so before moving on to Chapter 2. The choice, however, is yours. If you decide not to, that's okay, you can and should still read on, since I believe God will reveal Himself to you as you do.

Before you go on to Chapter 2, may I suggest that you read the following passages of Scripture and answer the related questions:

1. **Matthew 6:19-21:** What is one of the things man treasures most in life? Why does the Lord want you to trust Him for the money He blesses you with? What does what you do with your money say about you, and why is that important to God?

2. **Luke 16:11-12:** In what do you think you have to be faithful if

you are to receive true riches? Whose possessions do you have to be faithful with if you are to receive more? What does being faithful with another's "stuff" demonstrate?

3. **Matthew 6:24, 33:** How many masters can you serve at any one time? Why can't you serve more masters than verse 24 says that you can? What does it mean to seek God first, and why is that important? What does it tell God about us?

4. **Psalms 24:1:** Who is the owner of everything that exists? Who are the stewards of everything that exists? What is a steward, and why is being a good steward with your money important?

5. **Romans 8:28:** Why should you be confident after reading this verse that you can be a good steward over your money, even if you've messed up managing your money in the past?

6. **1 Corinthians 4:2 & Luke 16:10:** What does God really want from you? What is necessary in order for you to be a good steward? What do you have to do to demonstrate your faithfulness in order to be blessed abundantly by God?

7. **John 10:10 & 1 John 3:8:** What do these scriptures tell you about the devil? What do these scriptures say that Jesus has done to the works of the devil?

There's nothing wrong with having money,
as long as money doesn't have you.

Chapter 2

What Does God Say About Money?

Did you read the suggested passages listed at the end of Chapter 1? If you did, what did you learn and what questions do you still have? We'll do a recap of those passages and that should answer most of your questions, and perhaps inspire you to go back and read those passages if you didn't do so already. In this chapter I will continue to lay the foundation with some basic principles that you need to understand in order to fully understand the concept of Kingdom prosperity.

What do you think money is for, and why do you think God wants you to have it? Let's look at Matthew 6:19-21 to find the answer:

"Do not lay up for yourselves treasures on earth, where moth and rust destroy and where thieves break in and steal; but lay up for yourselves treasures in heaven, where neither moth nor rust destroys and where thieves do not break in and steal. For where your treasure is, there your heart will be also."

The first point you can take away from these verses is that money is the one thing man treasures most of all in life. Why? Because it takes money to get things done in this world, including what God wants to get done through you and me. God is the creator of all, however, and needs you to realize that He is your source for all you need in your life including but not limited to money. Even more important is the fact that God is really interested in your heart more than He is in what you have or what you are. He knows how much you treasure and value money, so if He can get you to give Him your money, He knows He has your heart. He then also knows that you truly realize that He is your source, and that you don't look to your job, the government, or other people as your providers.

The second point to take away from the Matthew passage is that where you give or put your money is an indication of where your heart is and who or what you really trust and identify as your source. Do you trust God or the world? No need to answer that right now; just meditate on it. Hopefully, when you finish this book, you will understand why you should trust God as your only source for money and everything else. You will also hopefully understand that if you handle and manage your money His way as a demonstration that you truly trust Him (even when what He is asking you to do doesn't make sense to you), God will honor and bless you with more money, while meeting all your needs, and after that your wants.

I asked you to read Luke16:11-12 at the end of chapter 1, which says:

"Therefore if you have not been faithful in the unrighteous mammon, who will commit to your trust the true riches? And if you have not been faithful in what is another man's, who will give you what is your own?"

If you can't be trusted to have faith in God and be a good steward over your worldly wealth (mammon) God gives you (that is, to manage your money the way God wants you to), how can you expect God to give you the true riches of His Kingdom, which are worth more than money and which money cannot buy – such things as love, peace, joy, righteousness, power and authority, divine health, the desires of your heart, fruitful relationships, and children. God promises all those things in His Word if you are faithful to Him? Being faithful with what is not yours, which in this case is God's (the money He has entrusted us to care for) demonstrates that you honor and respect God, in addition to trusting Him as your source. It also shows God that you desire Him as much as He desires you.

In Matthew 6:24 & 33 Jesus tells you that "No one can serve two masters; for either he will hate the one and love the other, or else he will be loyal to the one and despise the other. You cannot serve God and mammon. But seek first the kingdom of God and His righteousness, and all these things shall be added to you" You can't make both God and the things of this world (including money and wealth) the top priorities in your life, because eventually you are going to love one and hate the other, and God doesn't take second place to anyone or anything. That's why He tells you to seek Him first, and then He will provide for all of your needs. Part of your seeking God first is to trust Him as your source for all your needs, including all your financial needs, which means doing with and managing your money the way God directs you to do, no matter whether or not you agree or don't agree with what He tells you to do all of the time, or if what He tells you to do with your money doesn't make sense. If you try to rationalize everything God commands you to do, you'll get bogged down and never be all He wants you to be or have all He wants you to have!

The next verse I asked you to look at was Psalms 24:1: "The earth is the Lord's, and all its fullness, the world and those who dwell therein." The point to understand in this short verse is that God created everything and it all belongs to Him, not to you. Even the air you breathe is not yours, but rather it belongs to God, just like you, your family, and your money – it's all God's. You are an owner of nothing, but a steward of everything you have. We'll talk more about stewards and stewardship in later chapters, but for now understand that a steward is someone who is entrusted with something that belongs to someone else, and is charged with taking care of the something the way the owner wants.

Let's take banks, for example. You put your money in a bank, but it's not their money, it's yours. You give it to them to manage, protect, and increase it. At the end of the day, however, a bank is a steward over the financial resources you give them, and you expect banks to grow your money into more than when you gave it to them. In the same way, you are to be good steward over what God gives you, including the financial resources He gives you, managing them as He wants, not as you want.

Keep thinking about a bank. When they do a good job managing your money, what do you do? You give them more to manage. The better they manage, the more they get, and the bank is also able to share in the increase (return) you get on your money. It's the same way when God blesses you with financial resources. If you are an effective steward over that money, He will give you more. As you continue to be an effective steward over what He gives you, He gives more and more, and in the process all of your needs are met. After that, your wants that are not in conflict with His Word will also be met.

Now let's consider Romans 8:28: "And we know that all things work together for good to those who love God, to those who are the called according to His purpose." You might be asking, "How can I expect God to trust me to manage anything, let alone money, the way I've messed up my finances and perhaps many other things in my life?" This verse should give you confidence that no matter how many mistakes you've made with money in the past, God still wants both to give you a chance to demonstrate you trust Him as your source, and also to let Him know that you truly believe He can turn around any situation in which you find yourself. That truth should encourage you to try God's way, since He wants the very best for you. Why? Because He is your heavenly Father if you know Him through Christ.

Now let's take a look at 1 Corinthians 4:2: "Moreover it is required in stewards that one be found faithful." and Luke 16:10, "He who is faithful in what is least is faithful also in much; and he who is unjust in what is least is unjust also in much." God wants your heart, not your money, which is His anyway. As I mentioned earlier, because he knows how much man values money, He knows if you demonstrate your faithfulness to Him as your source for money, He will have your heart.

On the one hand, the verse from 1 Corinthians tells you it's necessary to be a good steward. On the other hand, the verse from Luke says you must first demonstrate your faithfulness with a little in order to be trusted with or have a chance to demonstrate your faithfulness with a lot. As you start to apply the biblical as well as practical principles you learn from this book, you will gradually change and turn around your financial situation. Therefore be patient, give it time, don't be discouraged, and trust God.

We've just begun to scratch the surface of what God has to say about money, but I think you can see that God has quite a lot to say about the subject. We'll cover many more verses that speak about what God has to say about money in later chapters, but I want to cover one more thing God says about money here in this chapter that has been a pitfall for many of us.

Have you ever heard people say, and maybe even said yourself, that money is the root of all evil? I'd venture to say most if not everyone has at one time or another. As a result many people have come to believe and many churches have taught that God doesn't want you to have a lot of money, that you are just to get by on a little, always struggling, that never having much is God's will for you. Well I am here to tell you that nothing could be further from the truth! The problem is many people have misquoted the Bible when they say money is the root of all evil, including some in the pulpit. The Bible actually says in 1 Timothy 6:10: "For the love of money is the root of all kinds of evil, for which some have strayed from faith in their greediness, and pierced themselves through with many sorrows."

The first part of the verse says the love of money is the root of all kinds of evil. It's not money that is evil, but the love of it. God wants to get money into your hands to accomplish what He wants to get done here on earth (more on this in Chapter 4). Money itself can't be bad or cause evil. The problem is when man starts to idolize money and make it the end rather than a means to an end. It's man's love of money that can manifest itself as "all kinds of evil" in our lives. That's why, as you saw in Matthew 6:19-21, God wants you to demonstrate to Him that you truly trust Him as your source for money. If you can let go of the control of the money you have and trust God to meet your needs, then He knows you can be trusted with more money to carry out His will on earth. And in the process, all of your needs will be taken care of (see Matthew 6:33).

Note what else 1Timothy 6:10 says – "for which some have strayed from faith in their greediness, and pierced themselves through with many sorrows." One's greed for money is the external expression of one's internal love of money, and really says to God that you don't trust Him (or need Him) to meet all of your needs. You can think, "The more money I have, the better I will be able to take care of myself." As the verse says, the love of money or greed demonstrates that you don't trust God as your source, that you don't have faith that if you do with your money what He wants you to do, God will supply all of your needs.

When you lose faith in God, you are no longer under His covering and you open the door for all kinds of evil to come into your life (including debt, lack, want and need). You pierce yourself as it were with "many sorrows," hardships and struggles. James 4:7 bears this out when it says, "Therefore submit to God. Resist the devil, and he will flee from you."

Another verse often misquoted or quoted in part, is found in this verse (James 4:7). Most people know the second half of the verse: "Resist the devil, and he will flee from you." They often overlook the first part, which says, "Therefore submit to God." We'll talk more about what submission means later, but if the verse tells you to submit to God so you can resist the devil, it also means that if you do not submit to God, then when you try to resist the devil, he won't flee from you. This is why when you don't have faith in God to do what he said in His Word He would do and to do what He's told you to do, you open the door for the devil to come in and take whatever you have despite your best efforts to stop him.

Remember that it says in the first part of John 10:10: "The thief does not come but to steal, to kill and destroy." I'm so glad that Jesus came so that I may have abundant life (the second part of John 10:10 - "I have come that they may have life, and that they may have it more abundantly") and to undo or destroy the works of the devil. As John also wrote in 1 John 3:8, "He who sins is of the devil, for the devil has sinned from the beginning. For this purpose the Son of God was manifested, that He might destroy the works of the devil."

The conclusion is that God doesn't look upon money as being evil or bad. If fact, He wants you to have as much of it as possible to expand His Kingdom on the earth and to have the abundant life He has promised you. It's important to realize that money is not the end, only the means, and in order to use it as God intends you need to have faith in Him and trust Him completely as your source. That doesn't mean you don't have to work. If fact, you are to work to support your family, those for whom God has entrusted you to care. You need to seek God and trust Him to guide you into the job He wants you to have, through which He can use and bless you.

As I close Chapter Two, here are some more passages along with questions for you to read and answer before going on to Chapter Three. Maybe you are tempted to jump right to Chapter Three and not read the scriptures or try and answer the questions. You are certainly free to do that.

Like anything else worthwhile, however, you can only get out of something what you put into it. Therefore I encourage you not to jump ahead, but rather take the time to read the passages below from your own Bible, and write down what God puts in your heart as responses to the questions. The insight you get will be helpful to you in your quest for Kingdom Prosperity as you learn how to be a successful financial steward.

Here are some more passages and questions to consider before moving on to Chapter 3:

1. **Romans 13:8:** What is the only thing you should ever owe anyone? Does God encourage or discourage debt? What should you do if you have any debt?

2. **Proverbs 22:7:** When you are in debt, what is it being like? Since Jesus has already delivered us from bondage, should you be in debt?

3. **Deuteronomy 28:1-2, 12:** Which of God's commandments are you to obey? What does God do when you obey His commandments? Does God see His children as borrowers or lenders?

4. **Deuteronomy 28:15, 43-44:** What happens when you disobey God's commandments? Is living a lifestyle of debt in obedience or disobedience to God's commandments? Is it ever permissible to be in debt? If it is okay to ever have some debt, can you give some examples?

5. **Proverbs 17:18:** Is it permissible to co-sign for someone else to get a loan? What is it that is so unacceptable about co-signing?

No debit is best,
but some may be necessary.

Chapter 3

What Does God Say About Debt?

Let's take one more chapter to lay the foundation before I share the meat of what God has shown me about kingdom prosperity and successful financial stewardship. In this chapter, I want to talk to you about debt.

What is debt? There are any number of definitions I can use, but there are two that I like. The first is that debt is something one person is obligated to pay another; the other is that debt is something owed that has to be repaid. The words obligated and owed both refer to a legal or moral commitment. Putting all this together, I define debt as it relates to financial stewardship as "a financial commitment that legally and morally must be repaid."

The financial commitment can be in the form of cash, credit or a loan, for which some sort of legal or moral agreement or contract has been made requiring the debt to be repaid. This may take the form of a mortgage note, a loan agreement, a credit card contract, or a verbal or written contract between two people. The legal or moral agreement can also be defined as a covenant, a term sometimes used to describe such agreements. A covenant in God's eyes is quite serious - a binding agreement between two or more parties that cannot be broken without penalty, injury or even death.

Debt is not something to be taken lightly and should be repaid according to the terms of the agreement behind the debt. Numbers 30:2 says, "If a man makes a vow to the Lord, or swears an oath to bind himself by some agreement, he shall not break his word; he shall do according to all that proceeds out of his mouth." Debt is like a vow or oath that binds one by the terms of the agreement and that shouldn't be broken. If you have a debt and do not repay it according to the agreement under which the debt was created, you have broken the Word of God and that amounts to sin.

It is clear then that if you have any debt, God expects you to repay it according to the terms under which the debt was created. But what does God say about having any debt at all? Romans 13:8 states, "Owe no one anything except to love one another, for he who loves another has fulfilled the law." According to this verse, God doesn't want you to owe anybody anything except love. It seems to say that God discourages debt. Therefore, ideally you should not create any debt for yourself. But if you do, you should pay it off and then do everything you can to stay out of debt. The problem is that debt has become a way of life in the world today. In fact, unless you have some debt that you are paying off, it is extremely difficult to establish good credit. Not only has debt become a way of life in the world, but also many people are "drowning" in debt with no or very little idea of how to get out of it.

We know that all good things come from God (see James 1:17), so all bad or evil things must not come from God but from the world system or the devil. It is clear that from God's perspective debt is not a good thing, so it must be of the devil - a convenient deception the enemy has used to bind many and get their focus and attention off the things of God. We see then that God doesn't want you to have any debt, but if you do, you should honor the agreement under which you incurred the debt and pay it off so you are no longer in debt.

Proverbs 22:7 tells us, "The rich rules over the poor, And the borrower is servant to the lender." Debt then is like being a servant or a slave to the person, company, or bank you owe, and is a form of bondage that Jesus has already delivered us from according to God's Word. God's will is for you not to be caught up in the bondage of debt.

In Deuteronomy 28:1-2, 12 God tells us:

"Now it shall come to pass, if you diligently obey the voice of the Lord your God, to observe carefully all His commandments which I command you today, that the Lord your God will set you high above all nations of the earth. And all these blessings shall come upon you and overtake you, because you obey the voice of the Lord your God.... The Lord will open to you His good treasure, the heavens, to give the rain to your land in its season, and to bless all the work of your hand. You shall lend to many nations, but you shall not borrow."

The first thing we see in these verses is that we are to obey God's commandments, all of them, not just the ones we like or prefer. When you do the Lord will abundantly bless you. We also see, however, that God sees His children as the lenders and not the borrowers. Therefore since one who has debt is a borrower, we as His children should not have any debt.

Deuteronomy 28:15, 43-44 goes on to say:

"But it shall come to pass, if you do not obey the voice of the Lord your God, to observe carefully all His commandments and His statutes which I command you today, that all these curses will come upon you and overtake you . . . . "The alien who is among you shall rise higher and higher above you, and you shall come down lower and lower. He shall lend to you, but you shall not lend to him; he shall be the head, and you shall be the tail."

One of the penalties for disobedience to God's commandments is bondage in ways we are not aware of, to people, principles or concepts we don't even know. One of God's commandments as stated in verse 12 is that we should be the lender and not the borrower. So if you live a lifestyle of debt, constantly borrowing from credit cards to pay for this or that, then you are disobeying God's commandment and the penalty is continually living a lifestyle of debt in bondage to others! Does this mean you shouldn't ever use credit cards? In an ideal world the answer is "Yes" but the society in which we live necessitates that from time to time you use credit cards as well as other forms of debt. The key is not to use credit cards beyond your means. If you use them, pay them off in full when the bill comes each and every month. This way you have not incurred any interest charges and are not in debt after you pay the bill off each month, thus meaning that you are not in bondage.

This brings us back to the statement at the beginning of this chapter I would like you to consider: "No debt is good, but some debt is necessary." Is it ever permissible to carry any debt? Given that you shouldn't incur any debt in the first place but realizing that some may be necessary from time to time, you need to make sure that what you use the debt for will produce an income or appreciate (increase in value over time) so you are in a position to pay the debt off. For instance, most people do not have enough cash on hand to purchase a home or even make upgrades to their home that has the potential to increase its value. Therefore it may be necessary to incur debt in that particular situation. The safeguard is for you to be a good steward and not borrow beyond what you are able to handle, which unfortunately many people have done.

Consider the mortgage crisis that made headlines several years ago when lending institutions loaned people money well beyond the means of those people to make the payments on their loans. This led to the second and third situations where it may be permissible to have some debt. The second scenario is when the value of what you use the debt for exceeds the debt incurred (what you owe), so that if need be you can use what you incurred the debt for to pay off the debt. The third is when the debt is manageable and you are able to build a plan into your budget to pay the debt off in a reasonable amount of time without putting undue stress on yourself financially nor put yourself into financial bondage.

I repeat that no debt is ideal since God does not want you to be in bondage to anyone. Don't take the scenarios I have described when debt may be acceptable as a license to run out and use credit or borrow money to simply acquire things you want as opposed to something you truly need.

There is a difference. If you must incur debt, do so only when what you use the debt for will increase in value (like the purchase of a house) or exceeds the value of the debt you incurred (such as, the value of the house you purchase exceeds the amount of your mortgage), and you are able to manage the debt and pay it off in a reasonable period of time without putting yourself in financial bondage.

Here are some general guidelines I have found helpful so that if you do have to incur debt, you do not put yourself into financial bondage:

1. Only borrow for things that you really need (You may need to purchase a new car, but based on your ability to pay for it, you may have to purchase a "mid-level" versus "high-end" vehicle until you are in a position in the future to afford a high-end vehicle);

2. Don't borrow more than you need, that you cannot manage to pay off in your budget, or an amount the repayment of which will put you in financial bondage;

3. Minimize the amount you borrow by making as much of a down payment as you can afford;

4. Be sure you can make more than just the monthly minimum payments each month in order to be able to pay off the debt early;

5. Determine how long of a payment period is necessary in order to

have a monthly payment that is within your budget but will you allow you to pay the note off early;

6. If collateral is required to incur the debt, be sure whatever the collateral is, that it is something you can do without;

7. Seek God's wisdom and direction before incurring any debt; and

8. After you have paid off a debt, rather than use the amount of what the monthly payment was to run right out and buy something else, put it toward another debt you may be trying to pay off or better yet, in your savings account.

These guidelines are not meant to be exhaustive nor are they in any order of priority. Some will be discussed in greater detail in later chapters. Since this chapter is addressing debt, however, I thought it would be helpful to share them here.

One last point needs to be made about another kind of debt I haven't yet mentioned. I made the mistake of incurring this type of debt when I was in my twenties, early in my professional career, and I had to learn the hard way that I should not have incurred it in the first place in spite of what the circumstances may have been at the time. Proverbs 17:18 says, "A man devoid of understanding shakes hands in a pledge, And becomes surety for his friend."

The point is that you should never, ever co-sign on a loan for someone else, unless you are in a position to completely pay off the loan in full should the person for whom you signed defaults. When you co-sign (which means you promise to repay the loan if the person for whom you signed cannot for any reason), you are the one who is on the hook for that loan, not the person taking out the loan! You are the surety for the person for whom you sign. This requires that you have the discipline and courage to say no, even to family members. You may really want to help them out, but you can most likely better help them by assisting them to learn how to be an effective steward over their financial resources. If need be, consider loaning them the money yourself if you have it, so you and they won't go into debt and if you can manage without the money you loan until they pay you back.

To summarize what God has to say about debt: He doesn't want you to incur any! If you can at all avoid debt, do so! But like many people you may not be in a position to live debt free until you learn how to better manage your money and become an effective steward over the financial resources God has blessed you with. If that's the case, be sure you are in a position to pay off the debt without putting financial strain on yourself, borrow wisely as discussed above, and only borrow if at all necessary for you needs and not your wants.

After you review the biblical passages in this chapter on your own, here are some suggested verses for you to read and questions to answer before moving on to Chapter 4.

1. **Deuteronomy 8:18:** What does the Lord give you so that you can obtain wealth? Why does the Lord want you to be wealthy? Why do you think God gives you something to be able to earn wealth, instead of just giving you wealth?

2. **Mark 16:15-16 & Luke 19:9-10:** What is God's covenant that He swore to man in the Old Testament? How is that covenant to be achieved according to the New Covenant? What is the purpose of God's covenant?

3. **Matthew 6:33:** What is God telling you to do in this verse, and how do you think what He's telling you to do relates to why God wants you to have wealth?

4. **Malachi 3:8-12:** Of what do these passages say you may have robbed God? What is it that you are to bring God, where are you to bring it, and why are you to bring it? Describe in your own words what the things you are to bring to God mean to you? What are the three things God says He will do if you bring to Him what He tells you to bring to Him?

5. **2 Corinthians 9:6-7:** What is God telling us we should do in these verses as it relates to giving, and how should we do it?

6. **Matthew 6:19-21:** What do these verses say about you according to what you do with your money?

7. **Leviticus 27 (whole chapter, emphasis on verses 26, 30, 32):** What is the tithe? Why is the tithe special to the Lord? Do you bring or give the tithe to the Lord?

8. **Hebrews 7:1, 2a, 4:** Is tithing an Old Testament or New Testament principle? Is tithing for us today, or a thing of the past?

9. **Hebrews 7:5-6:** How are you to bring the tithe to the Lord?

10. **Leviticus 27:31:** What is the penalty for not paying the tithe? To what can the penalty for not paying the tithe be compared?

11. **Numbers 18:12, Deuteronomy 26:10a:** When should you prepare your tithe? What part of your increase (income) should your tithe be?

12. **Exodus 36:3, Malachi 3:10, Galatians 6:6:** What is an offering? What does the offering do? Who can or should you give offerings to?

13. **Luke 12:33-34, Acts 10:1-4:** What are alms? And why are they important? What do alms do when combined with your prayers?

14. **2 Corinthians 9:6-8, Matthew 6:33, Matthew 6:21:** How should you give? What kind of a giver pleases God? If you seek God first in your

life, what does God promise you in His Word? What does where you

spend, place or invest your money tell God about you?

Part 2

Achieving
Kingdom Prosperity

Chapter 4

Tithes
and Offerings

Now we're ready to start our study of what Kingdom Prosperity and Successful Financially Stewardship are all about, beginning with what I call God's Financial Plan. Let's begin by looking at Deuteronomy 8:18a: "And you shall remember the Lord your God, for it is He who gives you power to get wealth."

The first thing we see here is that you are to remember God. If you want to be blessed by God you need to make Him first in your life, worship Him (acknowledge Him for who He is, which is God) and praise Him (thank Him for all He has already done, is doing and will do in your life), and live according to His Word. In 2 Chronicles 7:14 God says, "If my people who are called by my name, will humble themselves and pray and seek my face and turn from their wicked ways, then I will hear from heaven, and I will forgive their sin and will heal their land."

There's a problem in the world today and unfortunately it's also in many churches. We have gotten away from God, and not made Him the first priority in our lives. We chase after everything but God, all the things the world says makes someone successful like money, fame, fortune, and other things. If you truly want to have God move in your life and be blessed by Him in every area of your life including your finances, then you need to make Him the priority in your life, stop chasing after all the world says is good for you and will make you happy and successful, and seek God and His ways. If you do, He promises to forgive you and heal our land. If God is truly the Lord of your life, then you need to submit to His authority completely. This doesn't mean enslavement, because God wants His best for you, which you can have and includes "things" and "stuff" if you of your own free will chose to remember that he is our God, your Lord (Master and Ruler) and your Savior and follow His plan for your life.

We also see in this short verse that God gives us power to get wealth, but not the wealth itself. If God gives us power to get wealth, then that must mean God has all the wealth to give to us. When you use the power he gives to get wealth, you will receive the wealth that He has promised you. Romans 13:1 and Psalms 24:1 bear this truth out. Romans 13:1 says, "Let everyone be subject to the governing authorities for there is no authority except that which God has established." One of the definitions of authority in Merriam-Webster's Dictionary is "the power to influence or command thought, opinion or behavior." So then all power comes from God who said in Deuteronomy 8:18a that He is giving us that power to get wealth. Furthermore, Psalm 24:1 says, "The earth is the Lord's, and all its fullness, the world and those who dwell therein." The entire Earth and all its fullness belong to God, and I hope you agree that "all its fullness" would include all of the wealth in the world along with everything else. Therefore, both Romans 13:1 and Psalms 24:1 validate that God has all the power and all the wealth, and has given or given to us the power to get wealth as Deuteronomy 8:18a also says.

If all the wealth belongs to God, why doesn't God just give us the wealth directly instead of only giving us the power to get wealth? It's because there are conditions God has established for you to use His power to get wealth. One condition, as we saw in Deuteronomy 8:18a and 2 Chronicles 7:14, is that we need to remember God, put Him first in our lives and submit to His authority. The second condition is revealed in Deuteronomy 8:18b: ". . . that He may establish His covenant which He swore to your fathers, as it is this day." God's intent by giving you power so you can get wealth is not for you to use the wealth up on all the stuff you want, but rather to establish His covenant in this earthly realm. Given the condition of man and state of the world today, which promotes a "me first" attitude, a "gimme, gimme, gimme" attitude, we need to demonstrate to God that we can be trusted with the wealth, just we like we need to demonstrate to God that we can be trusted with anything He has promised us in His Word. And when God can trust you, He'll give you more of what you have demonstrated to Him He can trust you with.

It's similar to how we test our own children to see if they are ready for certain things before we give those things to them. If you demonstrate to God that you can be trusted to use the wealth he gives you the power to get as He wills, to establish His covenant in the earth realm, then all of your needs are taken care of, including all of your financial needs, according to Matthew 6:33: "But seek first the Kingdom of God and His righteousness, and all of these things shall be added to you." If you look at earlier verses in Matthew 6, 31-32, you will see that the "all of these things" in verse 33 refers to all of your needs. Using the financial blessings God gives you the power to get as God wills, demonstrates good stewardship on your part (taking care of or using God's stuff the way he wants you to) and that you can be trusted with more financial blessings.

What is the covenant God wants to establish in the earth realm through us with the wealth He gives us the power to get? In Mark 16:15-16 Jesus told His disciples: "And He said to them, 'Go into all the world and preach the gospel to every creature. He who believes and is baptized will be saved; but he who does not believe will be condemned.'" Furthermore Luke 19:9-10 says, "And Jesus said to him, 'Today salvation has come to this house, because he also is a son of Abraham; for the Son of Man has come to seek and to save that which was lost.'" As we've already seen in Matthew 6:33 we are told to "seek first the kingdom of God and His righteousness, and all these things shall be added to you." Sharing the gospel, the good news, the message of His kingdom and salvation to every nation of the world - that is the covenant God wants to use the wealth to establish on earth.

Therefore, if you put God first in your life and demonstrate through effective stewardship that you can be trusted to use wealth to establish His covenant on earth, then all your needs including your financial needs will be taken care of. What is this power that God gives to obtain wealth? The short answer is tithes and offerings. Let's examine these terms further.

Malachi 3:8-12 is a familiar passage of Scripture to most:

"Will a man rob God? Yet you have robbed Me! But you say, 'In what way have we robbed You' In tithes and offerings. You are cursed with a curse, for you have robbed Me, even this whole nation. Bring all the tithes into the storehouse, that there may be food in My house, and try Me now in this,' says the Lord of hosts, 'if I will not open for you the windows of heaven and pour out for you such blessing that there will not be room enough to receive it. And I will rebuke the devourer for your sakes, so that he will not destroy the fruit of your ground, nor shall the vine fail to bear fruit for you in the field,' says the Lord of hosts;' and all nations will call you blessed, For you will be a delightful land,'" says the Lord of hosts."

You see, giving tithes and offerings are not really optional. God expects you to bring the tithe, which is His, and to give offerings. When you are faithful to do so, God promises to open up Heaven and pour out an abundant blessing on you. And if you are good stewards with that blessing (using it to establish His covenant in the earth) God will prevent the enemy (the devil, Satan, the devourer) from robbing you of that blessing.

Now what is this storehouse God talks about in Malachi where you and I are to bring our tithes and offerings? It's not just any church or ministry where we might like for whatever reason. Rather, it's a local church or body of Believers where God has placed His name and that you call your church home. You can certainly give an offering to other ministries from which you are being blessed through their teaching you receive or the work they are doing for God, but your tithe should go to your local church where you receive the majority of your spiritual nourishment.

How do you know if a church is one where God has placed His name? The uncompromising Word of God should be going forth through biblical-based teaching, where signs and wonders occur, the gifts of the Holy Spirit are in operation, souls are being saved, and peoples' lives are being transformed. If none of these things are taking place, it's probably not a church where God has placed His name and you are probably not receiving the spiritual nourishment, teaching and training you desire and need to grow in the things of God.

You may ask: "What if I am not able to tithe at this point in my life?" The answer is that you really cannot afford **not** to if you want to reap the financial blessing God wants you to have. As discussed in Chapter 1, however, God is more concerned about your attitude toward tithing than the actual tithe. With God, it's always about the heart. 2 Corinthians 9:6-7 states, "But this I say: He who sows sparingly will also reap sparingly, and he who sows bountifully will also reap bountifully. So let each one give as he purposes in his heart, not grudgingly or of necessity; for God loves a cheerful giver."

If you are truly in a position where you cannot tithe (more on this in later chapters) but have a heart to tithe and an attitude that you know you should be tithing and earnestly desire to tithe, God will honor your heart. If you ask Him in faith he will give you seed (money) out of which you can sow (tithe) according to 2 Corinthians 9:10 "Now he who supplies seed to the sower and bread for food will also supply and increase your store of seed and will enlarge the harvest of your righteousness."

Although I've used these verses several times already, I can't stress enough that what you do with and where you put our money shows and demonstrates to God whether you trust Him or someone or something else. Matthew 6:19-21 explains it further when Jesus said, "Do not lay up for yourselves treasures on earth, where moth and rust destroy and where thieves break in and steal; but lay up for yourselves treasures in heaven, where neither moth nor rust destroys and where thieves do not break in and steal. For where your treasure is, there your heart will be also."

Let's summarize what we have talked about so far in this chapter.

1. God expects you to give (tithes and offerings). That's not an option for the believer.

2. The tithe is the power God gives you to obtain wealth.

When you give according to God's word to establish His Kingdom, you demonstrate to God that you are trusting Him as your source rather than anything else.

3. Your giving proves that God can trust you to be a good steward over the wealth He gives you.

4. How and to where you give is important because your attitude determines whether or not God accepts what you bring to Him (also more on this in future chapters).

Now that you know tithes and offerings are the key to God's Financial Plan, you need to be sure you understand just what tithes and offerings are. Let's start with the tithe. Leviticus 27:26, 30 and 32 states:

> "But the firstborn of the animals, which should be the Lord's firstborn, no man shall dedicate; whether it is an ox or sheep, it is the Lord's. . . . And all the tithe of the land, whether of the seed of the land or of the fruit of the tree, is the Lord's. It is holy to the Lord. . . . And concerning the tithe of the herd or the flock, of whatever passes under the rod, the tenth one shall be holy to the Lord."

The tithe is the *first* tenth of all of your increase, which today is mostly your income. And it is one tenth of the gross income, not the net, as these verses point out: "and all the tithe of the land" and "the tenth one shall be holy to the Lord." It doesn't say all or the tenth after any taxes you owe (or in today's society any other deductions that may come out of a paycheck).

Furthermore, the tithe is not limited to just income, but all of our increase as verse 30 says "all of the tithe of the land." This includes tithing on bank interest or gifts received (monetary or otherwise), anything else that represents financial increase. The tithe should also be our best as verse 26 points out "firstborn." In other words don't give God your leftovers, give Him your first and best. The tithe check should be the first check you write, not the last after you pay your bills and then see if you have enough left to give to God.

> Hebrews 7:1-2a and 4 says:
>
> "For this Melchizedek, king of Salem, priest of the Most High God, who met Abraham returning from the slaughter of the kings and blessed him, to whom also Abraham gave a tenth part of all . . . Now consider how great this man was, to whom even the patriarch Abraham gave a tenth of the spoils."

Note it says "Abraham gave a tenth part of all." This provides New Testament validation of what we read in Leviticus: the tithe is a tenth of all of our increase. Also note that these verses say the Abraham "gave" the tithe to Melchizedek. As Abraham was traveling from place to place, he met Melchizedek in the desert, recognized him as a high priest of God and gave him the tithe. The point as stated in Leviticus is that the tithe is holy and belongs to God. It's not optional as we've already seen. Therefore when you bring it to God you are in a sense paying it to God because it is holy to the Lord. In other words, the tithe is consecrated, set aside, or dedicated to the Lord (see Leviticus 27:30), since it is His anyway (see Psalms 24:1).

Hebrews 7:5-6 states:

And indeed those who are of the sons of Levi, who receive the priesthood, have a commandment to receive tithes from the people according to the law, that is, from their brethren, though they have come from the loins of Abraham; but he whose genealogy is not derived from them received tithes from Abraham and blessed him who had the promises.

Since we cannot physically bring or pay our tithes directly to God, we bring them to His high priest like Abraham did, those people today whom God has anointed over His people like Melchizedek in Abraham's day. Of course, they are the pastors and priests God has placed over the churches where he has placed His name for His people today.

Leviticus 27:31 tells us, "If a man wants at all to redeem any of his tithes, he shall add one-fifth to it." Once you are aware of the principle of tithing and are not obedient to it by not tithing or intentionally deciding to use all or part of the tithe for some other purpose, you still owe God the tithe plus 20% interest, the same as if you took out a loan at a bank because you are borrowing what is God's! This shows how sacred and holy God considers the tithe.

When I first learned about the principle of tithing, I didn't tithe for a number of years. When I caught the revelation of what the tithe represents to God (including among other things a demonstration to God that we trust Him as our source) and what Leviticus 27:31 said, however, I started tithing and rounding up to the nearest $5. I had no idea what the "principal and interest" was on the tithes I had not given to God, but figured that if I rounded up to the nearest $5 I would pay God what I owed Him over the course of my lifetime. There's no biblical basis for this, but I wanted to show God that I took the principle of tithing seriously and wanted to pay what I owed Him, and that by doing so I would demonstrate to Him that I truly trusted Him as my Source.

The Lord says in Numbers 18:12 and Deuteronomy 26:10a, "I give you all the finest olive oil and all the finest new wine and grain they give the Lord as the first fruits of their harvest." and "now I bring the first fruits of the soil that you, O Lord, have given me." Tithing is not a last minute thing you do. You should put your tithe aside as you receive increase and, as stated earlier in this chapter, the tithe check should be the first check you write or the first allocation out of your budget and not the last (budgeting will be discussed in detail in a future chapter).

I firmly believe you should prepare and pray over your tithes before you bring them to God, as the tithe should be the first and best of your increase and not your leftovers. Yes, you can give an additional amount as an offering if the Holy Spirit moves you to do so. The tithe should be in your budget, however, and there is no reason why you can't prepare and pray over it before coming to the house of God. Taking this approach says something to God about your heart and attitude toward tithing, in that you take it seriously, realize how holy it is to God, and that you trust Him as your source. We will look at some passages in the next chapter that address how you should bring your tithes to God.

Let me make a few more comments about tithing off of the gross or the net pay from one's paycheck. As I mentioned above, one should tithe based on the gross income instead of the net. Let's examine this concept to see if it is valid. When you accepted your current job position you signed on as it were for a certain number of dollars a year, let's say $78,000 per year, which is $1,500 per week. The $78,000 represents the increase you were expecting. Even though you signed on for $78,000, and assuming your net pay after taxes is $52,000 or $1,200 per week, some would say you should tithe off the $1,200 per week, the tithe totaling $120 per week, as that is what is actually coming to you.

Technically, that would be correct according to your employment agreement and the "law" of what the tithe is supposed to be, and I didn't see anything in Leviticus 27:32 that says the tenth is based on the gross or the net. You agreed, however, to an increase of $78,000 or $1,500 per week when you accepted your position, so tithing according to the "spirit" of what the tithe is to be would be a tithe calculated on $78,000 or $1,500 per week, which would be a $150 tithe.

In addition, knowing that God is more concerned about your heart than the amount of your tithe, what do you think it tells God about your heart if you decide to tithe off of the net instead of the gross? Doing so may be technically correct, but what does it say to God about where your heart is? That is a decision you must make and is between you and God. But as for me, I do not want there to be any doubt in God's mind where my heart is, so I choose to tithe off of the gross and not the net.

If you decide to tithe off of the net instead of the gross, what does that really mean? In the example above your $1,500 a week is reduced to $1,200 as a result of taxes. In addition, let's assume you have other deductions taken out of your pay check for a 401k plan, United Way, etc., further reducing your $1,500 a week down to $1,000 a week. What is the net pay you should be tithing off of? Some would say $1,000. I would suggest it should be based on the $1,200. Why? It is because you had control over that last $200 that was taken out of your paycheck, whereas you don't have much control over your taxes. You didn't have to have that last $200 automatically deducted. You could have received it in your paycheck and then made payments to your 401K, United Way or whatever the $200 might be for. But, you choose to have the $200 automatically deducted from your paycheck as a convenience to you. So before you tithe on the net, be sure to add back in any deductions over which you have control.

Finally, if you tithe off of the net instead of the gross and get a refund when you file your annual income tax return, you should tithe off that refund because you didn't tithe off of it when you originally received it in your paycheck. If you tithe off the gross, then any income tax refund you receive has already been tithed on, and while you are not bound to tithe off of it, I would suggest you consider making an offering out of the refund as a seed sown toward your next financial breakthrough.

Now let's talk about the meaning of an offering. In short, an offering is an act of worship and devotion given out of your own free will above and beyond the tithe. Exodus 36:3 says, "And they received from Moses all the offering which the children of Israel had brought for the work of the service of making the sanctuary. So they continued bringing to him freewill offerings every morning." Since the offering is given out of your own free will it has to be above and beyond the tithe since the tithe belongs to God, is owed to Him and isn't really a "freewill" offering. We bring God the tithe because we realize who He is, that the tithe is Holy and belongs to Him, to be obedient, and to demonstrate to God that we trust Him as our source. We give an offering, however, out of our own free will.

There are also different kinds or types of offerings you can give, to your church, another church or another ministry. As we have already read, Malachi 3:10 states, "Bring all the tithes into the storehouse, That there may be food in My house, And try Me now in this," says the Lord of hosts, if I will not open for you the windows of heaven and pour out for you such blessing that there will not be room enough to receive it." Notice this verse says to bring all the tithe into the storehouse not all of the tithe and offerings. Therefore, it must be permissible to give an offering to other churches or ministries that are doing the work of God in addition to your own church (which in this case I equate with the storehouse).

If you receive the majority of your spiritual nourishment from your church, then it would make sense that the majority of your offerings should go there as well (in addition to your tithes). One type of offering is to give into your church or another church or ministry to be used as they see fit to support the Kingdom work they are doing. Another type of offering would be an offering that is given to your church or another church for a specific purpose, such as a building fund or international missions fund.

Still another type of offering would be to someone you want to bless in recognition of the Kingdom work they have been doing or to honor how God has used them to speak into your life. This can even be something called a love gift for your pastor, which is in keeping with what Paul wrote in Galatians 6:6: "Let him who is taught the word share in all good things with him who teaches." That type of offering could also go to someone else in your church, or in another church or ministry who has spoken into your life or has made a difference in the lives of others through the Kingdom work they have done.

Alms are yet another type of offering that you can give. Luke 12:33-34 describes what alms are: "Sell what you have and give alms; provide yourselves money bags which do not grow old, a treasure in the heavens that does not fail, where no thief approaches nor moth destroys." Alms are a special type of offering given to help and relieve the needy, which as you see that God has commanded you to do as stated in Luke. God considers alms as a heavenly treasure that no one or nothing can destroy. Alms also accompany our prayers up before God as a memorial. It seems that alms puts our prayers right in front of Him as it were, bringing them to His immediate attention. This added attention can bring the manifestation of that for which we are believing God sooner rather than later as described in Acts 10:1-4:

> "There was a certain man in Caesarea called Cornelius, a centurion of what was called the Italian Regiment, a devout man and one who feared God with all his household, who gave alms generously to the people, and prayed to God always. About the ninth hour of the day he saw clearly in a vision an angel of God coming in and saying to him, "Cornelius!" And when he observed him, he was afraid, and said, "What is it, lord?" So he said to him, "Your prayers and your alms have come up for a memorial before God."

Finally, it is only when we begin to give offerings that we have actually begun to give. As C. Peter Wagner points out in his book *Discover Your Spiritual Gifts*, "True giving only starts with our offerings from the 90 percent God has given to us."[1] You see, the first 10 percent of your increase is not really yours to begin with. It's the tithe and belongs to God. That's why it helps to think about the tithe as being paid to God. It's from the remaining 90 percent that you actually start to give out of your own free will, which is why it is also helpful to think about your offerings as being given to God.

Now that you have a basic understanding of God's financial plan, the means through which He gets wealth to you to do the work of His kingdom on the earth and in turn to bless you abundantly, and what tithe and offerings are, we will examine how we should bring the tithes and offerings to God in Chapter 5. In preparation for this study, please read the following passages and answer the associated questions.

1. **Deuteronomy 26:1-15:** How should you prepare your tithes to bring before the Lord? How should you pray over your tithes?

2. **2 Corinthians 9:6-8; Matthew 6:33:** How should we give? What kind of a giver pleases God? If we seek God first in our life, what does God promise us in His Word? What does where we spend, place or invest our money tell God about us?

3. **James 4:1-10:** What is one of the reasons you don't receive what you ask God for? In what does friendship with the world result? Who does God resist, and who does He give grace to? What do you have to do in order for the devil to flee from you? Who does God lift up?

4. **Matthew 6:19-21:** What does where you put your money show God? How are tithes and offerings like having a bank account? How is your heavenly bank account different from your earthly bank account?

Chapter 5

Presenting Your Tithes and Offerings to the Lord.

A big mistake many people make after they first catch the revelation of God's financial plan is to run off and start tithing and giving, but doing it the wrong way and with the wrong motivation. When they don't see the increase in their lives they were looking for, they wonder why. One of the answers has to do with how you present your tithes and offerings to the Lord. How you give matters, in terms of both preparing to present your tithes and offerings and your motivation for giving. To study this concept I want to look at Deuteronomy 26:1-15, but we will look at it in bite-size chunks so we can chew and digest it properly.

Deuteronomy 26:1-3 says:

"And it shall be, when you come into the land which the Lord your God is giving you as an inheritance, and you possess it and dwell in it, that you shall take some of the first of all the produce of the ground, which you shall bring from your land that the Lord your God is giving you, and put it in a basket and go to the place where the Lord your God chooses to make His name abide. And you shall go to the one who is priest in those days, and say to him, 'I declare today to the Lord your God that I have come to the country which the Lord swore to our fathers to give us.'"

These verses reveal several things about God's financial plan. First, in verses 1 and 2 you are told to bring your "first produce" to the Lord. This reinforces what we learned in Chapter 4 about the tithe being the first and best we have - not what's left over - and that the tithe should be the first part of your increase that you set aside for the Lord.

Verse two also tells you that you should put the first produce in a basket. Since we do not live in an agricultural society as in Deuteronomy, the basket for us would be the collection containers at our local church into which we place our tithes and offerings, inside of an offering envelope. Most churches have offering envelopes available in the pews or at the ushers' station into which people can put their tithes and offerings. A good habit to get into (remember, this book provides both practical as well as biblical keys for successful financial stewardship) is to bring some offering envelops home from church to prepare your tithes and offerings each week before you bring them into the house of the Lord. It is not biblically incorrect to wait until you come into the Church to put your tithes and offerings into an envelope, but as you read on, you will see that bringing envelopes home will help you discipline yourself to faithfully prepare your tithes and offerings as God wants you to do.

Verse two goes on to say that you should take your tithes and offerings to the place where God has placed His name. This is the storehouse we learned about in Malachi 3, and in most cases is the local church where you receive the majority of your spiritual nourishment. Verse 3 tells you to bring the tithe and offering to the "priest". This is the pastor or spiritual head of your local church, or any other church leader who may from time to time be designated to receive the tithes and offerings of the people.

Deuteronomy 26:4-15 contains the meat of what it means to present your tithes and offerings to the Lord:

> "Then the priest shall take the basket out of your hand and set it down before the altar of the Lord your God. And you shall answer and say before the Lord your God: 'My father was a Syrian, about to perish, and he went down to Egypt and dwelt there, few in number; and there he became a nation, great, mighty, and populous. But the Egyptians mistreated us,

afflicted us, and laid hard bondage on us. Then we cried out to the Lord God of our fathers, and the Lord heard our voice and looked on our affliction and our labor and our oppression.

So the Lord brought us out of Egypt with a mighty hand and with an outstretched arm, with great terror and with signs and wonders. He has brought us to this place and has given us this land, "a land flowing with milk and honey"; and now, behold, I have brought the firstfruits of the land which you, O Lord, have given me.' "Then you shall set it before the Lord your God, and worship before the Lord your God. So you shall rejoice in every good thing which the Lord your God has given to you and your house, you and the Levite and the stranger who is among you.

"When you have finished laying aside all the tithe of your increase in the third year—the year of tithing—and have given it to the Levite, the stranger, the fatherless, and the widow, so that they may eat within your gates and be filled, then you shall say before the Lord your God: 'I have removed the holy tithe from my house, and also have given them to the Levite, the stranger, the fatherless, and the widow, according to all Your commandments which You have commanded me; I have not transgressed Your commandments, nor have I forgotten them. I have not eaten any of it when in mourning, nor have I removed any of it for an unclean use, nor given any of it for the dead. I have obeyed the voice of the Lord my God, and have done according to all that You have commanded me. Look down from Your holy habitation, from heaven, and bless Your people Israel and the land which You have given us, just as You swore to our fathers, "a land flowing with milk and honey."

These verses essentially tell you to pray over your tithes and offerings as you bring them to the Lord, and provides a model for doing so: thanking God for all He has done for you, bringing you from where you were to where you are, and for where He will take you to; rejoicing for every good thing the Lord has done for you, your family, your community and your church; declaring the tithe as holy and that you are bringing it (and/or offering) to Him, not having used any of it for your own purposes; and asking God to look down from heaven and bless you as He swore to do in His Word.

In most churches either before or after the tithes and offerings are presented the spiritual leader or his designate will pray over them corporately, on behalf of all of the people. However, as a practical matter and remembering that God is more concerned about the condition of your heart than the amount of your tithes and offerings, you should prepare to present your tithes and offerings at home each week before bringing them to the house of the Lord, by writing the check, placing the tithe and/or offering check in a giving envelope from your church, filling out the information requested on the front of the giving envelope, and praying over your tithes and offerings. Why should you do this?

First of all, you do this to let God know how much you are thankful for all He has done, is doing, and is about to do for you. Second, you should prepare your gifts as a demonstration to God that you are giving out of your heart and not out of any "ritual" or obligation to give (see discussion on 2 Corinthians 9 below). In this way you personalize your giving of tithes and offerings to the Lord, which you don't necessarily have the chance to do when presenting them in the house of the Lord (your home church). Yes, you bring tithes and offerings to the Lord in your home church, but you don't have the chance to individually confess what being able to bring the tithe and offering to the Lord means to you or to pray over them individually.

When I pray over my tithes and offerings at home, I also declare that I do truly trust the Lord as my source. The more often I say this, the more I will actually live this out in my life, trusting God as my source, as I exercise my faith by believing in my heart, confessing with my mouth and acting out my belief and confession that God is my source.

You should also do what I refer to as "name your seed," In other words, when you make out your offering envelop and pray over your tithes and offerings, ask God in your prayer and write on your envelope what you are believing Him for or need Him to do in your life. Many people are faithful tithers and givers, but still don't seem to receive the blessing God promises them in His Word. In addition to properly preparing the tithes to present to God and having the right motivation (discussed later in this chapter), may it be they don't receive their blessing because they don't ask? The last part of James 4:2 says, "Yet you do not have because you do not ask." While your heart, attitude and motivation for tithing and giving need to be right, that doesn't mean you cannot ask God for what you need. So as you prepare your giving/offering envelop and are praying over your tithes and offerings, let God know the blessing, breakthrough or miracle for which you are sowing. You can also write it on the envelope.

To summarize, a good process for preparing our tithes and offerings to bring to the house of the Lord, and incorporating some points from earlier chapters, is as follows:

1. Ask God for seed to sow so you can tithe and give offerings;

2. The tithe should be the first 10 percent of your increase, your first and best, which opens up the windows of heaven for you;

3. The offering is a freewill choice you make to give to the Lord above and beyond the tithe out of the remaining 90 percent, and determines the abundance of your blessing under an open heaven;

4. Write the tithe check first, before any other check is written;

5. Give an offering out of your own free will from the remaining 90%;

6. Put your tithes and offerings in the giving envelope used by your local church;

7. Name your seed;

8. Pray over your tithes and offerings at home, personalizing your prayer, thanking God for what He's done for you, rejoicing for all he has blessed you and your household with, letting Him know that you trust Him as your source, and asking Him to bless you as he has promised in His word;

9. Bring your tithes and offerings to the house of the Lord where He has placed His name, your home church, and present them to the Lord following the direction of the spiritual leader or his designate, and agree with the corporate prayer consecrating the tithes and offering of the people unto the Lord.

By the way, missing church service while on vacation or for some other valid reason is no excuse for not bringing the tithe and not giving an offering. You can mail them to your local church while you are away, or put them aside and bring them the next time you are in your local church. Since your tithes and offerings are needed each week to support the work of the Lord through your home church, better to mail them if you can't get there rather than wait until the next time you will be in your home church unless it's just a matter of a few days such as missing a Sunday service but being able to attend the next mid-week service.

There is also another option for presenting your tithes and offerings, and that is through online giving if your home church has this option available to you. This is especially helpful if you know you are going to be away and miss a service. Most online giving arrangements provide you the option to give online each time you give, or to set up automatic online giving at set times each week or month. I fully support online giving, but only use it myself when I am going to be away for an extended period of time. The reason is that online giving requires a high level of discipline to present your tithes and offerings as discussed above, especially if the automatic giving option is used. For me, it would be too easy with automatic giving to fall away from praying over my tithes and offerings at home each week as part of preparing to present them to the Lord, which I believe is the most important part of the preparation.

If you have the discipline to pray over your tithe privately at home in a way consistent with the preparation process discussed above, then by all means use the automatic online giving option if that is your choice. I also choose not to use automatic online giving because I would at some point forget to update my check register or credit card balance and could be out of balance. Online giving has a lot of benefits, but be sure your giving doesn't become impersonal or a matter of "rote" if you choose this option.

Let me share one more thing about the use of credit or debit cards to give online or in your church (some churches also offer an option on their giving envelopes to give by credit or debit card). You must have discipline! What do I mean by this? I mean that you need to be careful that you don't give what you don't have. The tithe is the first 10% of the income you have received and have in your account. If you tithe by credit card based on your gross income and don't have the amount you tithe or give as an offering, then you are not bringing the tithe or giving an offering as you are not giving out of your increase (the first 10% as the tithe, and if you are so moved, an offering out of the remaining 90%), and God will not honor that. All you are doing is "fronting", and trying to "look good." Trying to be recognized as a tither and giver when really you are not means that you are cheating God! In fact, not only won't God honor that and bless you, but also eventually you'll lose what you already have since you will be opening the door for the devil to come in to rob you and steal all that you have. I am not saying you cannot or should not use a credit or debit card to give, but make sure you are disciplined enough so that you are still giving out of your increase and not cheating God. Don't give what you don't have.

Now let's talk about the motivation behind our giving, as this matters as much as the preparation and presenting of our tithes and offerings. 2 Corinthians 9:6-8 reads:

> "But this I say: He who sows sparingly will also reap sparingly, and he who sows bountifully will also reap bountifully. So let each one give as he purposes in his heart, not grudgingly or of necessity; for God loves a cheerful giver. And God is able to make all grace abound toward you, that you, always having all sufficiency in all things, may have an abundance for every good work."

When you give, you need to do so with the right attitude and heart. You need to have the correct motivation when you bring the tithe and give an offering, or God may not accept it. Remember, God wants your heart as we learned in Chapter 2 when we studied Matthew 6:19-21. With God, it's always about the heart! Your heart and motivation must be a willingness and burning desire to support the Kingdom work on earth out of your love for who God is, regardless of what He may have or have not done for you. Remember Deuteronomy 8:18 tells you that God gives you power (bringing the tithe and giving the offering) to get wealth to establish His covenant, not to get done what you want to get done unless what you want to get done is consistent with God's covenant.

Matthew 6:33 validates what Paul wrote in 2 Corinthians 9:6-8 when Jesus tells us, "But seek first the kingdom of God and His righteousness, and all these things shall be added to you." If you read the verses before verse 33, you will see that "and all these things shall be added to you" is talking about all of your needs. If you put God first, catch the revelation of who He is, have an attitude that it is a privilege to sow into the Kingdom of God and want to willingly come under or be obedient to the authority of God's will, to seek first His Kingdom instead of all of your selfish needs and wants, have a desire to serve and please God for all He has done for you just as little children do to please their earthly fathers, then your heart is right and all your stuff (needs and the wants consistent with God's word) will be provided to you!

If it still isn't clear to you that God is more concerned about the condition of your heart when it comes to your motive for being obedient to His Word (including your giving), James 4:1-10 will certainly help make it clear for you. Let's look at James 4:1-5 first:

> "Where do wars and fights come from among you? Do they not come from your desires for pleasure that war in your members? You lust and do not have. You murder and covet and cannot obtain. You fight and war. Yet you do not have because you do not ask. You ask and do not receive, because you ask amiss, that you may spend it on your pleasures. Adulterers and adulteresses! Do you not know that friendship with the world is enmity with God? Whoever therefore wants to be a friend of the world makes himself an enemy of God. Or do you think

that the Scripture says in vain, "The Spirit who dwells in us yearns jealously?"

One of the reasons we don't receive the blessings, breakthroughs or miracles we need in our lives is because of our selfishness. Asking for things that we want but don't need, things the world craves, things to satisfy our flesh and our desires. In other words, we put our needs and the things we want before God. As we just saw in Matthew 6:33 and 2 Corinthians 9:6-8, we need to put God first so His will can be done, not ours. When we do, our needs will be met as well. Seek Him first. Show Him we can be trusted with a little so he will give us more!

James 5:6-10 goes on to say that we need to humble ourselves before God, realize both who He is and that we are nothing without Him, comprehend that all we have comes from Him, and willingly come under His authority. When we do, we will see God move in our lives, our prayers will be answered, and breakthroughs and miracles will come into our lives. We will also have God's power operating in our lives so when we command the devil to get out of our lives, he will have to flee!

> "But He gives more grace. Therefore He says: 'God resists the proud, but gives grace to the humble.' Therefore submit to God. Resist the devil and he will flee from you. Draw near to God and He will draw near to you. Cleanse your hands, you sinners; and purify your hearts, you double-minded. Lament and mourn

and weep! Let your laughter be turned to mourning and your joy to gloom. Humble yourselves in the sight of the Lord, and He will lift you up (James 4:7-10 NKJ)."

Look at the same verses from the Message Bible:

"Where do you think all these appalling wars and quarrels come from? Do you think they just happen? Think again. They come about because you want your own way, and fight for it deep inside yourselves. You lust for what you don't have and are willing to kill to get it. You want what isn't yours and will risk violence to get your hands on it. You wouldn't think of just asking God for it, would you? And why not? Because you know you'd be asking for what you have no right to. You're spoiled children, each wanting your own way. You're cheating on God. If all you want is your own way, flirting with the world every chance you get, you end up enemies of God and his way. And do you suppose God doesn't care? The proverb has it that "he's a fiercely jealous lover." And what he gives in love is far better than anything else you'll find. It's common knowledge that "God goes against the willful proud; God gives grace to the willing humble.""

God cannot make it any clearer than that. You don't get when you ask for because you ask and give for the wrong reasons. You want your own way and what you want, sometimes things you have no business asking for. You want to have one foot in the world and one foot in the Kingdom. Well, you can't have it both ways, because with God it's all or nothing. *The Message Bible* goes on in James 4:7-10 to say:

"So let God work his will in you. Yell a loud no to the Devil and watch him scamper. Say a quiet yes to God and he'll be there in no time. Quit dabbling in sin. Purify your inner life. Quit playing the field. Hit bottom, and cry your eyes out. The fun and games are over. Get serious, really serious. Get down on your knees before the Master; it's the only way you'll get on your feet. (MSG)"

You need to be serious about your relationship with God, get your heart and motivation right so you can submit to His will, and then and only then will you see God move in your life. When you have a right heart and motivation to give into the Kingdom so God's will can be done and not yours, when you use the little He gives you to further His Kingdom on earth so He will give you more, then you can have the financial breakthroughs for which you've been crying out to God, and so much more.

God wants your heart, and doesn't need your money! After all, it's all His anyway. In the world, however, money can be the most difficult thing to let go of. If you choose to part with your money with the right attitude and motivation, it shows God you truly trust Him as your source and He will take care of everything you need. Just like the tithe, your attitude toward giving offerings speaks to God about your heart as well, and determines whether or not He will accept your tithes and offerings, because it's the condition of your heart that matters to God, not the amount of money you give.

Now you may be saying. "That's all well and good, but I can't afford to tithe right now and give an offering. I don't have anything to tithe with or make an offering." I believe you cannot afford not to tithe and give offerings if you want to be blessed by God both financially and otherwise. You need to start where you are. If you have any type of income at all, I would start tithing off that, no matter how small it may be. If you do so with the right motivation, God will bless you with more. Then you may say, "I haven't managed my money very well and need every cent I have coming in right now to provide for my family." If that's the case, I've got good news for you. I will let you see it for yourself in 2 Corinthians 9:10-11:"Now may He who supplies seed to the sower, and bread for food, supply and multiply the seed you have sown and increase the fruits of your righteousness, while you are enriched in everything for all liberality, which causes thanksgiving through us to God."

If you truly do not have anything you can tithe or give right now, but your heart is right and you have the right motivation and truly want to be able to tithe, then just ask God for something (seed) to sow (tithe and offerings) and, according to these verses, He will give you seed to sow. Just be sure you use it to tithe, and don't give in to the temptation of using it for things you've been going without and want but which you don't really need or can get along without for a little while longer. Trust God! Have faith in Him, for He never fails, only people do.

Another way to look at presenting your tithes and offerings to the Lord is that you are making a deposit into your heavenly bank account according to Matthew 6:19-21, which says:

> "Do not lay up for yourselves treasures on earth, where moth and rust destroy and where thieves break in and steal; but lay up for yourselves treasures in heaven, where neither moth nor rust destroys and where thieves do not break in and steal. For where your treasure is, there your heart will be also."

Presenting your tithes and offerings to the Lord is one way you make deposits into your heavenly bank account, laying up treasure for yourself in heaven where it will last forever. That way when you go to God in prayer you've got something in the bank of heaven that can't be destroyed and upon which you can draw or make withdrawals when you need to through prayer. Those withdrawals may be not only for needed financial blessings, but also for any need you have in an area of your life or the lives for which you are interceding with God. If you don't make deposits into your heavenly bank account, however, then you don't have anything to draw upon or take out when you really need it.

Verse 21 also tells you that where you put your money is where your heart is, and as we learned earlier, God is really after your heart. Tithing and offerings demonstrate that you truly trust God as your source and that He truly has your heart. Finally, if you have not managed your money as you should have for an extended period or just recently and are now living with the consequences, I've got more good news for you. In the next chapter, we are going to start looking at how to manage your money and be effective stewards over it. I encourage you to keep reading.

Before we move on, however, here are some passages for you to read and some questions to consider in preparing yourself for our study on effectively managing your money in Chapter 6:

1. **Matthew 25:16-25:** Of what are these verses a good example? What happens when you follow the example in these verses, and when you don't? What does following the example in these scriptures demonstrate to God?

2. **Luke 16:1-2:** What are we all going to talk about with God eventually? What happens when you don't take care of God's stuff the way he wants you to?

3. **Luke 12:42-47:** What do these verses tell you about the rewards and consequences of being or not being an effective steward?

Part 3

Principles of Stewardship

Chapter 6

Taking Care of God's Stuff God's Way.

In the next four chapters we are going take a journey to learn what effective, biblically-based financial stewardship is all about. We will study four areas that I have found to be keys to successful financial stewardship. In this chapter we will learn what stewardship is, in Chapter 7 we will learn about developing financial priorities, in Chapter 8 we will cover the basics of budgeting, and in Chapter 9 we will talk about faith and discipline. Let's begin by looking at a basic definition of what stewardship is, and look at a few examples.

Various versions of the dictionary define stewardship in a different ways, but they all state that stewardship involves:

- taking care of something of value that belongs to someone else;

- the careful and responsible management of something confidently committed to ones care by another;

- a trust or confidence granted to someone for profitable use;

- administering the property, house, or finances, of another; and

- the responsible overseeing and protection of something considered worth caring for and preserving.

If you look at the definition of a steward, you would again see a number of definitions. The one I personally like is a person who administers anything as the agent of another or others. Another definition specifically related to finances says a steward is "a person who manages another's property or financial affairs."[2] The point is that being a steward and practicing stewardship involve taking care or watching over something that belongs to someone else, or taking care of other people's "stuff." As it relates to the things of God, including financial prosperity, practicing stewardship involves taking care of God's stuff.

Being a good or effective steward, however, is more than just "babysitting" or taking care of God's stuff or the stuff He has entrusted to others who in turn have entrusted it to you. It's taking care of God's stuff the way He wants you to take care of it so that when you return it to Him, it's of greater value than it was when He entrusted it to you. If we look at a few natural and biblical examples, this will become clear to you.

When you rent an apartment and put down a security deposit, the landlord entrusts you with that apartment while you live in it, and expects you to keep it in good condition. If you do, you get the security deposit back when your lease is up, or you are able to renew the lease. If you don't take good care of the apartment, you don't get your security deposit back, won't be able to renew your lease, and may be asked to leave early and be charged for damages to the apartment.

When you deposit your hard earned money at a bank, into a savings account, money market or some other interest bearing account, you are entrusting your money to that bank, expecting them to manage it wisely so that when you are ready to make a withdrawal, there is more in it than when you first deposited it. If the bank does a good job, you will most likely reward them and put more money into the bank. If the bank does not do a good job, you will most likely withdraw your money and look for another financial institution that will be a more effective steward over your money. In the first instance, you were a good or poor steward over your apartment. In the second, the bank was a good or poor steward of your deposits.

We see this concept in the Jesus' parable found in Matthew 25:14-30.

It's rather long, but I think it's important for you to see it all:

> For the kingdom of heaven is like a man traveling to a far country, who called his own servants and delivered his goods to them. And to one he gave five talents, to another two, and to another one, to each according to his own ability; and immediately he went on a journey. Then he who had received the five talents went and traded with them, and made another five talents. And likewise he who had received two gained two more also. But he who had received one went and dug in the ground, and hid his lord's money. After a long time the lord of those servants came and settled accounts with them.

> So he who had received five talents came and brought five other talents, saying, 'Lord, you delivered to me five talents; look, I have gained five more talents besides them.' His lord said to him, 'Well done, good and faithful servant; you were faithful over a few things, I will make you ruler over many things. Enter into the joy of your lord.' He also who had received two talents came and said, 'Lord, you delivered to me two talents; look, I have gained two more talents besides them.' His lord said to him, 'Well done, good and faithful servant; you have been faithful over a few things, I will make you ruler over many things. Enter into the joy of your lord.'

> Then he who had received the one talent came and said, 'Lord, I knew you to be a hard man, reaping where you have not sown, and gathering where you have not scattered seed. And I was afraid, and went and hid your talent in the ground. Look, there you have what is yours.' But his lord answered and said to him, 'You wicked and lazy servant, you knew that I reap where

I have not sown, and gather where I have not scattered seed. So you ought to have deposited my money with the bankers, and at my coming I would have received back my own with interest. So take the talent from him, and give it to him who has ten talents.'

'For to everyone who has, more will be given, and he will have abundance; but from him who does not have, even what he has will be taken away. And cast the unprofitable servant into the outer darkness. There will be weeping and gnashing of teeth.'

This parable explains an excellent example of effective stewardship, which is managing something entrusted to you to take care of on someone's behalf in the way they want you to take care of it. Two of the master's servants who were effective stewards didn't just hold on to the talents (weighted sums of money) their master gave them, they doubled the amount they had to present to their Master when he returned. And they were rewarded accordingly, with recognition, the promise of being given even more to care for, and being invited to come into the joy of their Lord (Master).

When you are an effective steward and do a good job of caring for what has been entrusted to you, you are rewarded. Similarly, as you see with the third servant who was given one talent and simply held on to it out of fear, he was not rewarded and even lost the talent the master had entrusted to him. Being a good steward demonstrates to God that you honor and respect what He has given you, and that you trust Him as your source. Consequently, God will bless you with more since He knows you can be trusted to take good care of what he blesses you with, not squandering it all on yourself. If you take care of God's stuff His way, He will take care of all of your needs as we have already studied in Matthew 6:33.

There are two other important points from which you can catch the revelation of stewardship in this passage of Scripture. You see in verse 15 that the master gave each of the three servants an amount of money consistent with the ability each one had. In other words, the master knew what each servant was capable of – that one servant could be trusted with and grow five talents, another two and another one. The point is that God will never entrust you with something he hasn't given you the ability to do something with, and especially if you have been negligent to develop that ability. This is often why it is such a long time before you receive the blessing after you have sown faithfully into God's kingdom work. It is because either you don't have the ability to handle that for which you are asking, or more likely, you have the ability but haven't developed it to the point where God knows you can handle it and be an effective steward. For example, if you've done a bad job managing your money and have lost most or all of it, while at the same time sowing and asking for a financial breakthrough that has not come, it's not because God hasn't heard your prayer but rather because you need to acquire and develop the skill of fiscal management, budgeting and monetary discipline. When you do, your answered prayer for a financial breakthrough will manifest in your life.

The other point from the Matthew 25 passage is that you should walk in faith according to what God has told you to do. That is, you need to believe what God said, confess it out of your month and act on what God said and directed you to do. All too often we don't do that and the result is that the answer to our prayer is delayed. One of the major reasons why we don't do what God expects us to do is fear, which is the opposite of faith. When you are afraid, you are not believing God can do what he said He would do or that we can't do what God said we can do or told us to do, just like the servant who had been given the one talent in Matthew 25:25. God is a God of faith, and responds to your acting by faith on His word. If God told you to do it, then you need to do it and trust God for the results.

According to the concepts found in the Matthew 25 parable, if you want to be blessed financially, you need to carefully and responsibly manage the financial resources God has already entrusted to you the way He desires. Because this is such an important concept, I want to look at three more examples of effective stewardship, not all in the financial realm.

The first has to do with how we raise our children, who are a gift from God. Psalms 24:1-2 states, "The earth is the Lord's, and all its fullness, the world and those who dwell therein. For He has founded it upon the seas, and established it upon the waters." This tells you that everything belongs to God your money, children, jobs, trials and tribulations, good times, bad times, and even the air you breathe. We are owners of nothing, but stewards of everything. When God blesses a family with children, he expects the child's parents to be effective stewards by raising the children to fear the Lord. By doing so, the children will live as men and women of God when the child is of age and out on his or her own.

When children are first born, they are like a clean white board with no writing on it. The parents write things on that board to help script the child's life according to God's will and values. When God gave the child to the parents the child was a baby and knew nothing, could do nothing, say nothing understandable, or even feed itself. Parents who are effective stewards teach their child all these things, also raising the child in the things of God according to Proverbs 22:6: "Train up a child in the way he should go, and when he is old he will not depart from it." When children are of age and ready to go out on their own, they have been equipped to pursue a godly lifestyle, trained to let the Lord guide them as they should go.

The second and third examples have to do with how you manage the financial resources God has blessed you with, and how you do at that will determine if God will bless you with more. The first example is found in Luke 16:1-2:

> "He also said to his disciples: 'there was a certain rich man who had a steward, and an accusation was brought to him that this man was wasting his goods. So he called him and said to him, 'what is this I hear about you? Give an account of your stewardship, for you can no longer be steward.'"

We see in these verses that when you are entrusted with something, you eventually have to give an account to the owner of what you did with the entrustment. The steward in these verses squandered his rich master's goods away, was "called on the carpet" for it, and never entrusted again with any of his master's goods. He forfeited his right to be a steward.

The same holds true when God entrusts you with His goods including money. You will eventually have to give God an account of what you did with them. You can be like the good servants we read about in Matthew 25 and grow what God gave you into more than it was when He gave it to us, which includes using the financial blessing you receive from God the way He wants. Or you can be like the wicked servant in Matthew 25 or the lazy steward here in Luke 16 and maintain or squander away what God gives you. The choice is yours but you need to be willing to live with the consequences of your decision. I don't know about you, but I want to be a good steward over what God gives me so I can demonstrate to Him that I can be trusted with more, and in the process have all of my needs met as well. If you choose not to be a good steward, then you will probably never have much more than you have now, and have only yourself to blame.

The last example of stewardship I want to quickly review comes from Luke 12:42-47:

> And the Lord said, 'Who then is that faithful and wise steward, whom his master will make ruler over his household, to give them their portion of food in due season? Blessed is that servant whom his master will find so doing when he comes. Truly, I say to you that he will make him ruler over all that he has.' But if that servant says in his heart, 'My master is delaying his coming,' and begins to beat the male and female servants, and to eat and drink and be drunk, the master of that servant will come on a day when he is not looking for him, and at an hour when he is not aware, and will cut him in two and appoint him his portion with the unbelievers. And that servant who knew his master's will, and did not prepare himself or do according to his will, shall be beaten with many stripes.

On the one hand, we see in these verses that if you are submitted to the authorities you are under and are good stewards over what you have been entrusted to watch over, you will be blessed (verses 42-44). On the other hand we also see that if you aren't submitted and are not good stewards, you will be punished (verses 45-47), and subject to God's wrath, which is something to which I don't ever want to be subject.

I think we have a good understanding of what stewardship and being a steward is all about. I hope you see why good stewardship is so important to being financially prosperous in the kingdom of God. As with everything else in the Kingdom, God is more concerned about your heart than about your money. Being a good steward demonstrates to God that you trust Him as your source, and that you have fully consecrated and sanctified yourself unto Him. Good stewardship shows God that you put His will above your own in how you handle the financial blessings He gives you. Kingdom prosperity is not just about knowing God wants you to prosper, following His financial plan and bringing the tithe and offerings to Him with a right heart and attitude, but it's also about what you do after you receive the corresponding blessing in return.

This is where many people have missed the boat. They've paid the tithe, given offerings and even done so with a right heart. When they received a blessing in return, however, they thought they had "arrived" and didn't need God anymore, consequently squandering the blessing away while thinking they could get more money on their own. After they did this, they found the doors God had opened for them with the initial financial blessing were closed. Why? Because they weren't good stewards over that which God had blessed them.

In other instances, they paid the tithe and gave offerings with a right heart, but when they received a blessing in return, it was not what they were expecting, so they are dissatisfied with it, take it for granted, are upset with God, or go back to trying to accumulate wealth on their own. God blesses you incrementally. That is, each time you follow His financial plan, He blesses you, not just again, but with more, and the next time with more, and so on as you demonstrate you can be trusted to be a good steward over more and more.

This is how you become financially prosperous in the kingdom of God. If God gave you all you need or want the very first time you followed His financial plan and trusted Him as your source, and you haven't learned how to handle that much money yet in a Kingdom way, you will most certainly squander it. A lot of lottery winners you hear about hit the jackpot and a year or two later are broke. God wants you to be able to grow in Kingdom prosperity to further His work on earth, be a blessing to others, and have an abundant life. He desires for you to prosper and teach others how to do the same. It takes time and anything worth waiting for is worth fighting for.

Let's summarize what we have learned about stewardship:

Russell Gross

- Stewardship is taking care of someone else's stuff the way they want you to take care of it;

- It's a trust or confidence granted to someone for profitable use;

- Looking after someone else's possessions and returning them in a better condition than when they were entrusted to you;

- Doing and taking care of what the authority you are under told you to do or entrusted you with the way they commanded you to, so that it grows into something more (better) than it was when you received it;

- The careful and responsible management of something confidently committed to your care by another; and

- Stewardship is not just babysitting something belonging to someone else, but nurturing, watering and growing it.

God wants you to be a good and effective steward over that He entrusts to you in all areas of life. He gives you tools and resources and expects you to take care of them and use them the way He wants and commands. When you do, He blesses you with more tools and resources and in other ways in areas of your life. When you don't, He doesn't. It's that simple. It's up to you to focus on your financial condition or money. This is what true stewardship is about – taking care of God's stuff God's way for God's purposes.

89

In the next several Chapters we will examine what effective stewardship looks like and how to be an effective steward. Before you go on to Chapter 7, however, here are some suggested passages and questions for your consideration:

1. **James 1:5; Psalms 119:24; & Hebrews 4:12:** What do these verses tells you? How can these verses help you to become an effective financial steward?

2. **Psalms 37:30-31; Proverbs 6:20-22; & Proverbs 15:22:** What do these passages say about seeking counsel with respect to financial priorities? What are some of the characteristics to look for when seeking wise counsel?

3. **Leviticus 19:31:** About what does this verse tell you to be careful when seeking wise counsel?

4. **Psalms 1:1; Proverbs 8:11; Proverbs 19:20 & Proverbs 12:15:** What do these verses say you should do when you receive wise counsel?

Chapter 7

What Are Your Financial Priorities?

In this chapter we discuss what effective financial stewardship looks like, how to establish your financial priorities and the concept and development of a personal budget. Before you develop your budget, you should determine what your financial priorities are without respect to their cost and your income. Why is that? If you don't have an idea of where you want to end up financially, you will never get there. Also, if you look at your current financial limitations, you will never get to where you want to be. As my pastor constantly reminds us, your past doesn't have to dictate your future. Where you've been and are financially doesn't mean you can't change that position for the better in the future. Don't let your past or current financial situations hinder either your goal setting or your future priorities.

Your financial priorities do not spell out how you will achieve them, but represent what is important to you and what you want your budget and overall financial plan to achieve. There is no one way to determine what your financial priorities are, and most people cannot develop their financial priorities without some help. Where is a good place to start?

I would suggest you start working on your financial priorities with prayer. As I mentioned in earlier chapters, James 1:5 says "5 If any of you lacks wisdom, let him ask of God, who gives to all liberally and without reproach, and it will be given to him." In addition, Psalms 119:24 states, "Your testimonies also are my delight And my counselors" and Hebrews 4:12 says, "For the word of God is living and powerful, and sharper than any two-edged sword, piercing even to the division of soul and spirit, and of joints and marrow, and is a discerner of the thoughts and intents of the heart." God's Word is intended to be your guide and counselor for how you live your life.

By the way, if you are a married couple, determining your financial priorities should be done together, so that you are in full agreement of what they are. While husbands and wives should pray together daily. this is an area about which they should specifically pray. In fact, the ideal situation is for a husband and wife to pray about and agree on their financial priorities before entering marriage. Even if you did not do this before you were married, it's never too late to do so, especially if you are struggling with your finances.

After you've prayed and gotten wise counsel from the Lord, start making a list of what you think your financial goals or priorities are, writing down anything and everything that comes to mind. When making your list, be sure to consider all of the principles covered in the previous chapters, things like savings, giving and investments. This is not going to be your final list of priorities, but rather a starting point.

After you have your initial list of financial goals, it's time to get some help to become knowledgeable about things that may be important you hadn't previously considered, re-thinking some goals that should not be priorities, consolidating goals that are redundant, and prioritizing your financial goals. There are many resources available to help you do that, including other people who are financial planners and experts. Psalm 37:30-31 teaches that "The mouth of the righteous speaks wisdom, and his tongue talks of justice. The law of his God is in his heart; none of his steps shall slide." Proverbs 6:20-22 says:

"My son, keep your father's command, And do not forsake the

law of your mother. Bind them continually upon your heart; Tie them around your neck. When you roam, they will lead you; when you sleep, they will keep you."

Proverbs 15:22 states, "Without counsel, plans go awry, but in the multitude of counselors they are established" When you seek God's counsel regarding your financial priorities, also seek His guidance on who else to consult. You need to be sure when you ask other people for help that they know what they are talking about. Seek out people you know who are either financially successful, or least are better off than you are.

Let me add another reason why you should seek God's counsel on who to consult as you develop your financial priorities. Not only do you want to seek people who are knowledgeable and have some success financially, but also people with whom you don't have a problem sharing a lot of personal information. As a rule of thumb, you may want to think twice before going to close family or friends, other than to ask them for referrals for advisers who may be helpful. This is also why a lot of people use outside financial advisors who are skilled to help them develop their financial goals and plans for achieving them.

I have used a financial advisor for years to help fine tune my financial goals and develop plans to achieve them, more specifically my investment plans, which I then used as additional input to develop my budget. You also have to do your homework before choosing a financial advisor or anyone else from whom you seek financial advice as Leviticus 19:31 warns: "Give no regard to mediums and familiar spirits; do not seek after them, to be defiled by them: I am the Lord your God." Those you are most familiar with may not be the best people for you to consult.

When you do seek counsel and guidance from God and others regarding your financial priorities, you must be willing to listen to what you are told, and not dismiss their advice just because you don't like it or don't want to follow it. Psalms 1:1 says, "Blessed is the man Who walks not in the counsel of the ungodly, Nor stands in the path of sinners, nor sits in the seat of the scornful." Proverbs 8:11 warns, "For wisdom is better than rubies, and all the things one may desire cannot be compared with her." Proverbs 19:20 says, "Listen to counsel and receive instruction, that you may be wise in your latter days"; and finally Proverbs 12:15 says, "The way of a fool is right in his own eyes, but he who heeds counsel is wise." This doesn't mean you have to follow everything anybody tells you. Just have an open mind and weigh what you are told without any preconceived notions.

There are other resources and tools available online and in book stores to help develop your financial priorities. One I recently became aware of and is the called the Final Four developed by the National Endowment for Financial Education (NEFE) and Financial Planning Association (FPA). This service came online a few years ago so you could go through the process just like college basketball fans do during the NCAA March Madness each year when they fill out their brackets. The Final Four Financial Plan is based on a list of 32 financial priorities developed by financial experts. This list may not contain all the right priorities for you, which is why the online tool was developed so you can develop your own final four. Based on people using the online tool, the top final four financial priorities for 2012 were:

1. **Live Within Your Means.** It shouldn't surprise you this was the overwhelming top choice among financial planners and advisors. Spending less than you earn and living within your income is the best way to ensure you meet your financial goals.

2. **Protect Yourself with Adequate Insurance.** Ensure your financial security by having adequate insurance coverage in place for health, disability, long-term care, auto, homeowners and renters to protect yourself and your assets.

3. **Build an Emergency Savings Account.** Prepare for the unexpected by having this important reserve. Keep this account

separate from your savings and aim for three- to six-months of living expenses. Starting with a small reasonable goal—as little as $500—will help springboard you toward this goal. Your tax return may provide a great way to start.

4. **Establish Life Insurance for Wage Earner(s).** Protect your family by having adequate life insurance for all wage earners. Having a policy in place to cover six to 10 times your gross annual income will ensure financial security for your loved ones if you are not there to provide for them.

The full list of 32 financial priorities are defined on the web site and ranked by financial experts who developed them are as follows:

1. Live within your means
2. Protect yourself with adequate insurance
3. Build an emergency savings account
4. Establish life insurance for wage earner(s)
5. Understand short and long-term goals
6. Communicate with family
7. Know amount of debt/have a payoff plan
8. Ensure job security
9. Perform a regular financial check-up
10. Spend less than a third of income on housing
11. Have a will/financial and health-care power of attorney
12. Know your partners' financial personality
13. Pay yourself first
14. Take advantage of savings programs available at work

15. Calculate what you will need for retirement
16. Understand the time value of money
17. Experience change before it happens
18. Spend wisely
19. Understand financial terminology
20. Save at least 10 percent of what you earn
21. Make tax time financial planning time
22. Understand investing risks vs. returns
23. Budget for anticipated holidays/celebrations
24. Understand income
25. Use credit responsibly
26. Manage service providers
27. Understand and take advantage of workplace benefits
28. Prepare a financial emergency kit
29. Protect financial documents
30. Track spending
31. Keep up on maintenance
32. Pull credit report

Let me make a few comments about the last priority, pulling your credit report, before discussing the online tool in more detail. This is something I would advise you to do as part of the process of determining your financial priorities, instead of it being a financial priority. Your credit score gives you a starting point that you use to help determine your financial priorities. No matter if your credit rating is excellent, good, fair or poor, knowing it will go a long way to help you determine what kind of leverage you have when you want to get credit, be it to take out a mortgage, buy a home, or get a credit card. The rating and analysis behind the rating will point you toward what you need to do to improve your credit, which may include:

1. Reduce the amount and/or kinds of debt you have;

2. Do a better job of paying bills on time, which can then be built into a budget (more on that in the next chapter); and

3. Reducing debt.

It's a good idea to check your credit report at least annually to see what if anything has changed and where you stand. If you are trying to improve your credit, you may want to check it more frequently, say every three to six months, after your action plans have been in place for a while.

The Final Four online tool is really easy to use. Each of the 32 priorities are grouped into four brackets with 8 priorities in each category:

- Growing Your Money

- Protecting What You Have

- Learning And Talking About Your Money

- Spending Wisely

Just like the March Madness brackets, the eight financial priorities within each cluster are paired off. You then select your choice for each match-up to go to the next round. For example, in the Growing Your Money cluster or bracket the match-ups are:

- Build Emergency Savings vs. Define Savings Goals

- Start Saving Early vs. Expand Retirement Portfolio

- Use Employer Savings vs. Calculate Retirement Needs

- Pay Yourself First vs. Assess Investment Risk

The winners of each match-up go on to the next round until you reach the final four - your top four financial priorities based on use of this tool, with the finals resulting in your number one financial priority. The results are not necessarily what you go with as your financial priorities, but one additional input along with other sources available to you including those discussed above.

For example, using the final four tool at www.financialfour.org, my final four financial priorities came out as:

1. Expand Retirement Portfolio

2. Rein In Debt

3. Maintain Adequate Insurance

4. Use Debt Responsibly

"Rein In Debt" became my number one financial priority. Your final four will not necessarily be the same as mine, but as I went through this process, it confirmed another thing I thought to be true: Your financial priorities are a function of where you are in life, how old you are, and what your core values are. Lastly, as mentioned, whatever your final four are, the result is one more input to consider in developing your financial priorities.

One additional resource I will mention is the Crown Money Map, created by Howard Dayton of Crown Financial Ministries, to help you achieve financial freedom. The map is laid out as a journey you take to true financial freedom. The first step takes you through a process to determine what your life purpose and life goals are, including some biblical foundational principles, with supporting scriptures, that you should keep in mind as you progress through each step of your journey to financial freedom. There are then six destination steps, each of which you need to describe before you go to the next destination. Each destination step is supported by Scripture and focuses on such things as emergency savings, paying off credit cards, paying off consumer debt, saving for major purchases, buying a home, saving for investing and paying off your home mortgage. The destination steps relate to what we will cover in the next chapter, but the initial steps of determining your life purpose and life goals are more tools you can use to determine your financial priorities. For more information on the Crown Money Map, go to www.crownmoneymap.org.

No matter what method or process you use, the point of this chapter is to highlight the importance of having financial priorities established before jumping into the process of developing a budget. If you have not done that yet, I highly recommend you do so before starting on your budget.

Now you are almost ready to put together a budget, which is what we will do in Chapter 8. Before you go on to Chapter 8, however, here are some suggested scriptures and questions for your consideration:

1. **2 Chronicles 31:14, Matthew 22:15-22, Matthew 25:26-28, Luke 18:22, Acts 4:36-37**: What do these passages tell you that you are to do with the resources God blesses you with, including your financial resources?

2. **1 Chronicles 28:11, Proverbs 16:9, 2 Corinthians 1:15-20, 1 Kings 6:38**: What do these verses speak to, and what connection is there to the first set of passages above?

Chapter 8

The Budget: Roadmap to Successful Financial Stewardship

Before we get into the specifics of what is budget is and its purpose, I thought it might be helpful to take a look at what God has to say about budgeting. When I researched the word budget in the Bible, I could find no specific reference for that word. However, I did find a number of verses that speak to things we can do with the resources God gives us, and the importance of "planning." I had you look at those passages at the end of chapter seven, but let's take a closer look at them as we begin this chapter on Stewardship 103.

1. **2 Chronicles 31:14, 15b** – "Kore the son of Imnah the

Levite, the keeper of the East Gate, was over the freewill offerings to God, to distribute the offerings of the Lord and the most holy things . . . to **distribute allotments** to their brethren by divisions, to the great as well as the small."

This passage speaks to making distributions of allotments out of freewill offerings, which first have to be given before allotments can be made. We should make freewill offerings out of our financial resources, which we talked about in much detail in Chapter 5.

2. **Matthew 22:15-22** – "Then the Pharisees went and plotted how they might entangle Him in His talk. And they sent to Him their disciples with the Herodians, saying, 'Teacher, we know that You are true, and teach the way of God in truth; nor do You care about anyone, for You do not regard the person of men. Tell us, therefore, what do You think? Is it lawful to **pay taxes** to Caesar, or not?' But Jesus perceived their wickedness, and said, 'Why do you test Me, you hypocrites? Show Me the tax money.' So they brought Him a denarius. And He said to them, 'Whose image and inscription is this?' They said to Him, 'Caesar's.' And He said to them, 'Render therefore to Caesar the things that are Caesar's, and to God the things that are God's.' When they had heard these words, they marveled, and left Him and went their way."

We see in these verses that we should pay taxes to whom they are due.

3. **Matthew 25:26-28** - "But his lord answered and said to him, 'You wicked and lazy servant, you knew that I reap where I have not sown, and gather where I have not scattered seed. So you ought to have **deposit**ed my **money with** the **bankers**, and at my coming I would have received back my own with

interest. Therefore take the talent from him, and give it to him who has ten talents.'"

Here we see that we can deposit some of our financial resources with bankers, which today we would refer to as investing or saving.

4. **Luke 18:22** – "So when Jesus heard these things, He said to him, 'You still lack one thing. Sell all that you have and **distribute to the poor**, and you will have treasure in heaven; and come, follow Me.'"

Doctor Luke tells us we should give some of resources (which would include our money) to the poor. In other words, give alms as we also talked about in Chapter 5.

5. **Acts 4:36-37** – "And Joses, who was also named Barnabas by the apostles (which is translated Son of Encouragement), a Levite of the country of Cyprus, **having land, sold it**, and brought the money and laid it at the apostles' feet."

These two verses speak to buying and selling land, which requires money to do.

The point from these examples is that there are allocations or allotments you should be making from financial resources you have. There are many more than just those noted here, including the tithe which we covered in Chapter 5. How can you go about doing that in a way that demonstrates effective stewardship? The following verses give insight into that:

6. **1 Kings 6:38** - And in the eleventh year, in the month of Bul, which is

the eighth month, the house was finished in all its details and **according to all its plans**. So he was seven years in building it.

7. **1 Chronicles 28:11** - Then David gave his son Solomon **the plans** for the vestibule, its houses, its treasuries, its upper chambers, its inner chambers, and the place of the mercy seat;

8. **Proverbs 16:9** - A man's heart **plans** his way, but **the Lord directs his steps**.

9. **2 Corinthians 1:15-20** - "And in this confidence I intended to come to you before, that you might have a second benefit— to pass by way of you to Macedonia, to come again from Macedonia to you, and be helped by you on my way to Judea. Therefore, when I was planning this, did I do it lightly? Or the things I plan, do I plan according to the flesh, that with me there should be Yes, Yes, and No, No? But as God is faithful, our word to you was not Yes and No. For the Son of God, Jesus Christ, who was preached among you by us—by me, Silvanus, and Timothy—was not Yes and No, but in Him was Yes. For all the promises of God in Him are Yes, and in Him Amen, to the glory of God through us."

Each of these last four passages speak to plans, determining how you will do something before you do it, or as Merriam Webster defines plans: "a set of actions that have been thought of as a way to do or achieve something."

In order to be effective stewards over the financial resources God has blessed you with, before you run out and start doling out money here and there any old way, you need a plan. Not just any old plan, but one that incorporates all of the principles of Kingdom prosperity this book has covered thus far.

What is a budget? There are many definitions but they all revolve around having a plan for allocating resources according to the principles of Kingdom prosperity. A budget includes knowing what you have coming in, your assets, what you owe, liabilities, and a plan for matching up assets and liabilities. A budget is a guide, not a hard-and-fast rule. You should follow it, but be flexible enough to adjust it as unforeseen circumstances arise.

Assets that go into a budget consist of your salary and wages including any bonuses you might earn, but also include any other income you may have from rental properties, investments, interest bearing accounts, sales of any kind, and the monetary value of gifts you receive. In other words, your assets include all of your increase. Liabilities include things such as your tithes, utility bills, mortgage or rent payments, balances on credit cards or lines of credit, loans, car payments, insurances (home owners, auto, medical), cable TV, taxes, weekly grocery shopping, gasoline for your car, clothing, housekeeping and other homeowner-related services, and any other bills you may have, In other words, anything you owe or must pay.

A budget should also include other items such as dining out, savings, offerings and charitable donations, subscriptions (for magazines, etc.), entertainment, vacations, children's college education, investments, and anything else you can think of that you may wish to spend money to obtain. Budgets should include any and all income and increase you expect to receive and any and all expenditures you expect to have to pay.

With that general description of what goes into a budget, how do you develop a budget? To answer that question I am going to share how I develop my budget using a simple Excel spreadsheet, and incorporating as I go along all of the principles of Kingdom Prosperity. You can create the same spreadsheet on your own computer based on the template I will discuss shortly, or make copies of the template and develop your budget long-hand.

I want to preface the process by saying there are many different ways to develop a budget, and many computerized tools you can use to do so. Some may be better than others including the process and tool I am about to share with you, but most will get you there. I am simply sharing with you what I know and what has worked for me over the years. So let's get started.

On the following page is the template I use to develop my budget. The number of columns and rows will depend on what you put in your budget

Item	Due Date	Balance	Minimum Payment	Month/ Day	Month/ Day	Total
						$0
						$0
						$0
						$0
						$0
						$0
						$0
						$0
						$0
Total						$0
Net Pay						$0
Balance						$0
Cum. Balance						$0
Gross Pay						$0

and how far out you want to budget. Let's do a review of it's headings:

1. **Item** – a list of things to go in your budget as discussed above.

2. **Due Date** – The day/month a payment is due, or the frequency of when a payment is due.

3. **Balance** – The amount currently owed for each item.

4. **Min. Paymt**. – The minimum amount that has to be paid whenever payments are due.

5. **Mo/Day** – The dates when you plan to make payments, which are usually when you are paid, which could be weekly, semi-monthly or bi-weekly. Depending on how you are paid, you can add as many columns as you like to budget for one week, one month, two months, etc. I have found that for me budgeting two months at a time works best. For the purposes of this example, however, we will budget for just one month.

6. The **total column** is an automatic calculation done in Excel of the entries for each item in each row under all of the day/month columns, to let you know how much in total you are paying out for the period for which you are budgeting. If you set up an Excel spread sheet, create a formula to sum columns E through J in column K for each row, and format columns C through G for currency, which will result in the $0.00 in column K until other entries are added. You may need to enlist the services of someone who knows how to use Excel, but I assure you it will be a great help to learn for yourself.

The row headings at the bottom of the template are as follows:

1. **Total** – The sum of all of the entries in rows 2-10 under columns C-G.

2. **Net Pay** – Your net pay any time you receive income or what actually gets deposited in your account, including any non-income increase that you receive like interest or rent from properties (just add it to your net pay for that period).

3. **Balance** – The difference between all of the payments and allocations you plan to make each time you are paid and your net pay, row 12 minus row 11 for columns E through G.

4. **Cum. Balance** – The same as item 3, but cumulatively for each pay period for the time frame you are budgeting.

5. **Gross Pay** – The gross amount of income you receive each time you are paid (Gross pay from income plus the amount of any non-salary increase that you receive during that budgeting period).

With these definitions, let's go on to the next step, which is entering all the payments you will be making the under the **Item** column. The examples on the next page are not all inclusive, but will give you an idea of some of the items or categories of expense for which you should be budgeting.

Let me make a comment here if you are questioning why I am going through all of this explanation. It is not because I think you don't know anything, but everyone reading this book is not going to be at the same level of knowledge and experience with respect to budgeting. I want to be sure we are all on the same page. If you already know all, most or some of what I am explaining, please bear with me for the benefit of those who do not.

Next, list all of the payments, expenses or allocations you need to make in Column A. Again, this list of payment items in column A has intentionally been kept short due to space limitations, but is representative of the types of payments you should consider in your budget. You should start out by listing everything you can think of that you may have to pay or want to spend.

Most of the categories I have listed in the example on the next page are self-explanatory, but a few may need further explanation:

1. **Tithe** – Always list this first, since this belongs to God and should be the first thing you pay.

2. **Insurances** – It's probably best to list each type of insurance separately, but for this example I have lumped life, auto, homeowners and health insurance together as a single item.

3. **Gas/Electric** – Like insurances, it is best to list these separately, but for this example I lumped them together.

4. **Self** – Always allocate some money for yourself in case of emergencies or other unbudgeted expenses that may come up, especially those that arise on the spur of the moment.

5. **SAV** – It's a good idea to budget what you plan to save each payday. This is savings that would go in your savings account beyond anything else you use to save such as the next item, IRA.

6. **Seed** – This is a "seed account" for you to put money aside to sow "seed" or make special offerings, such as when there may be a guest speaker at your local church you want to bless, or to give a special offering as the spiritual leader of your local church may suggest.

7. **Offerings/Blessing** – Like insurances and utilities, it's best to list these separately, but for this example I have lumped them together. Offerings are your giving to the Lord above and beyond the tithe, and Blessings is money available to bless someone who speaks into your life, someone whom you admire for the way they serve the Lord, or someone you are witnessing to, or "just because."

Some other items I have in my budget which may or may not apply to your situation and which I did not included due to space limitations include:

1. **Timeshare** - Annual fees that have to be paid if you are a timeshare owner.

2. **Capital Campaign** - Fund-raising initiatives you commit to support, be it at your church or some other organization with which you are involved.

3. **Yard Maintenance** - Outdoor home services you may hire others to do such as lawn mowing, spring cleanup, snow removal, etc.

Item	Due Date	Balance	Minimum Payment	Month/Day	Month/Day	Total
1. Tithe						$0
2. Telephone						$0
3. Mortgage						$0
4. Credit Cards						$0
5. Car Payment						$0
6. Groceries						$0
7. Insurances						$0
8. Gas/Electric						$0
9. Cable TV						$0
10. Self						$0
11. Savings						$0
12. Property Tax						$0
13. Subscriptions						$0
14. Seed						$0
15. Offerings/Blessings						$0
16. Gasoline						$0
17. Clothes						$0
18. Internet						$0
						$0
Total						$0
Net Pay						$0
Balance						$0
Cumulative Balance						$0
Gross Pay						$0

4. **TVG** - *TV Guide*, if you happen to subscribe to it as I do.

5. **ADT** - A home security/alarm service.

6. **IRA** - Additional IRA payments you make beyond what you automatically have deducted from a paycheck.

7. **Charities & Ministries** - Giving to community-based and faith-based ministries outside of your local church.

8. **House Cleaning** - For maid service or any type of special cleaning you need to have done at your home.

9. **Long-Term Care Insurance** – Coverage beyond basic health and life insurance policies for items that may not be covered like home care, assisted living, nursing home, etc.

Don't be overly concerned if at first you may have missed something. As you go further in this process and even after your initial budget is developed, you will always be making adjustments and fine tuning your budget, adding or deleting items as necessary. For example, if you like to travel you should budget for that, be it for pleasure or perhaps for a missions trip. Whatever you might have a need to fund should be in the budget.

The next step in the process is to fill in columns B, C and D with the dates any payments need to be made, current balances and any minimum payment requirements as depicted in the next Table. Note that balances are only listed for items where you still owe something. Even though you may

Item	Due Date	Balance	Minimum Payment	Month/ Day	Month/ Day	Total
1. Tithe	as paid	n/a	10% gross pay			$0
2. Telephone	16th	n/a	$100			$0
3. Mortgage	10th	$50,000	$500			$0
4. Credit Cards	10th	$2,000	$200			$0
5. Car Payment	15th	$7,500	$350			$0
6. Groceries	weekly	n/a	$150			$0
7. Insurances	1st	$5,400	$900			$0
8. Gas/Electric	25th	n/a	$200			$0
9. Cable TV	16th	n/a	$150			$0
10. Self	as paid	n/a	$150			$0
11. Savings	monthly	n/a	$250			$0
12. Property Tax	1st day of 2nd month of qtr.	$3,000	$750			$0
13. Subscriptions	annual	$200	$120			$0
14. Seed	as paid		$25			$0
15. Offerings/Blessings	as paid	n/a	$50			$0
16. Gasoline	weekly	n/a	$50			$0
17. Clothes	as needed	$2,500/year	$200			$0
18. Internet	21st	n/a	$25			$0
						$0
Total						$0
Net Pay						$0
Balance						$0
Cumulative Balance						$0
Gross Pay						$0

be billed for a certain item each month, if you are current on your payments, there would be no balance. The balance column however, can also be used to list amounts normally required for any quarterly or annual payments so when the time to make the payment nears, you can budget for it.

I think most of the entries are again self-explanatory, but let me cover some that may not be:

1. For several items there is no balance, but a **minimum payment** is listed. That means you are current on your payments, but the next time the bill is due there is a minimum payment. In addition, some of the minimum payments are self-imposed, such as for savings (SAV), which is not required but represents what you would like to pay or put into your savings account.

2. **Subscriptions** – The balance and minimum payment are both $200, which means all of your magazine subscriptions collectively total $200, and when the bills are received the total amount to renew each subscription is due. It might be easier for items like this to list each subscription separately. To simplify the example I am working through, I listed them all as a single item. The same holds true for any house cleaning services you may use.

3. The entry for **clothing** is an estimate on how much you might average on clothing each year, with the minimum amount representing something you would like to put aside each month for clothing, even though you might not spend that amount each month.

Some of the balances and amounts entered may look out of line, since you spend a lot more or less for some of the items listed. Don't get hung up on the amount, but rather grasp the concept. The more you work with the budget using this tool or some other method, the more comfortable you will become filling in the balance and minimum payment columns. Remember, it's your budget, so you can use the entries for whatever works best for you.

One last check you should make before going to the next step is to make sure that you have included any outlay of money that relates to your financial priorities. For example, first and foremost is your tithe, the first and best 10%, which is why I recommend you list it first. If saving for your children's schooling is a financial priority, you should list it in the budget. The same would hold true if having an emergency fund is a priority. For me, emergencies are taken out of my savings. But if you are not at the point where you might not remember that, you may want to list emergency funds as a separate budget item. Obviously, the tithes and offerings are a priority in order to follow God's financial plan.

You should get in the habit of listing budget items that relate to your financial priorities first in your budget. If you've spent time properly developing those priorities, you should list them high on your budget item list. Also, don't get distracted by thinking about how much you owe, or that you may not have enough to pay all of your bills. You are still laying the foundation in your budget, and the time to address shortfalls or a surplus of financial resources will come later in the budget development process.

Once you have everything listed and have cross-checked your list with your financial priorities, make one last check to make sure the list reflects your financial priorities, along with the Foundational Principles of Kingdom Prosperity, God's Financial Plan and the concepts of biblical stewardship. When you've done all of that, your list is complete for now.

The next step is to fill in the information for your **Net Pay** and **Gross** pay at the bottom of the budget template. The example below shows that you are paid on the 1st and 16th of the month as a number of people are. These dates are listed across the top of the template in the example below. Whatever your pay period dates are, they should be listed. You will also add the year, but I have left that out in the generic example. In this example we are assuming you make $72,000 annually, $6,000/month or $3,000 per pay period, and you net 70% of your gross pay based on taxes and other deductions you have taken out of your paycheck.

Note the $300 that shows up for tithe. In setting up your Excel spread sheet, you should place a formula in the tithe cells so that the 10% of your gross pay is automatically calculated. If the amount comes out with dollars and cents or is less than a multiple of $5, I suggest you round up to the nearest $5. Also note that the spreadsheet should set up formulas in Column I, automatically summing Columns E and F.

Believe it or not, the easy part of developing your budget is complete. Now it's time to move on to the more challenging aspects of the budget - determining how you want to allocate what you have coming in. I continue

Item	Due Date	Balance	Minimum Payment	April 1st	April 16th	Total
1. Tithe	as paid	n/a	10% gross pay	$300	$300	$0
2. Telephone	16th	n/a	$100			$0
3. Mortgage	10th	$50,000	$500			$0
4. Credit Cards	10th	$2,000	$200			$0
5. Car Payment	15th	$7,500	$350			$0
6. Groceries	weekly	n/a	$150			$0
7. Insurances	1st	$5,400	$900			$0
8. Gas/Electric	25th	n/a	$200			$0
9. Cable TV	16th	n/a	$150			$0
10. Self	as paid	n/a	$150			$0
11. Savings	monthly	n/a	$250			$0
12. Property Tax	1st day of 2nd month of qtr.	$3,000	$750			$0
13. Subscriptions	annual	$200	$120			$0
14. Seed	as paid		$25			$0
15. Offerings/Blessings	as paid	n/a	$50			$0
16. Gasoline	weekly	n/a	$50			$0
17. Clothes	as needed	$2,500/year	$200			$0
18. Internet	21st	n/a	$25			$0
						$0
Total						$0
Net Pay				$2,100	$2,100	$0
Balance						$0
Cumulative Balance						$0
Gross Pay				$3,000	$3,000	$0

with our example below with the first pass, which should be done based on what you ideally would like to pay, without respect to what you have coming in. Allocations are based on the timing of when bills are due, along with the minimum payments due. It will take several passes before your initial budget is complete, so please take a look at the example on the next page, and then we'll explain what it all means.

So what does this first hypothetical pass at developing a budget tell us? If we look at the **Total**, **Net Pay**, **Balance** and **Cum. Balance** rows at the bottom, which with the exception of the **Net Pay** row are calculated automatically by the Excel spread sheet with formulas in Rows 39, 41 and 42, under Columns E through K, we see the following:

1. Looking at the **Cum. Bal** (row 42) under column I, we see that over the course of April there is a shortfall of $745 to cover all of the currently budgeted April expenses.

2. Looking at Balance (row 41) under columns E and F we see that there is not enough income to cover the currently budgeted expenses for both April 1 and April 16 ($210 and $535, respectively) with the cumulative shortfall again being $745 (row 42, columns F and I).

The next step is to balance the expenses you would want to pay during April, with the challenge being to reduce the amount of expenses to be paid in the first April pay period by at least $210 and cumulatively through the second April pay period by at least $745, so that there is never a cumulative shortfall. There is no magical formula for doing this, and it is more of an art than a science, and may require several attempts. In making revisions to the first pass of the budget, you need to make sure that any bills that have to be paid by certain dates are actually paid, so that your credit score is not impacted by any underpayments or late payments.

Item	Due Date	Balance	Minimum Payment	April 1st	April 16th	Total
1. Tithe	as paid	n/a	10% gross pay	$300	$300	$600
2. Telephone	16th	n/a	$100	$0	$100	$100
3. Mortgage	10th	$50,000	$500	$500	$0	$500
4. Credit Cards	10th	$2,000	$200	$200	$0	$200
5. Car Payment	15th	$7,500	$350	$0	$350	$350
6. Groceries	weekly	n/a	$150	$150	$150	$300
7. Insurances	1st	$5,400	$900	$650	$250	$900
8. Gas/Electric	25th	n/a	$200	$0	$200	$200
9. Cable TV	16th	n/a	$150	$0	$150	$150
10. Self	as paid	n/a	$150	$150	$150	$300
11. Savings	monthly	n/a	$250	$125	$125	$250
12. Property Tax	1st day of 2nd month of qtr.	$3,000	$750	$0	$600	$600
13. Subscriptions	annual	$200	$120	$10	$10	$20
14. Seed	as paid		$25	$25	$25	$50
15. Offerings/Blessings	as paid	n/a	$50	$50	$50	$100
16. Gasoline	weekly	n/a	$50	$50	$50	$100
17. Clothes	as needed	$2,500/year	$200	$100	$100	$200
18. Internet	21st	n/a	$25	$0	$25	$25
Total				$2,310	$2,635	$4,945
Net Pay				$2,100	$2,100	$4,200
Balance				($210)	($535)	($745)
Cumulative Balance				($210)	($745)	
Gross Pay				$3,000	$3,000	$6,000

The second pass at developing a budget on the next page is the first attempt at trying to balance the budget, with what was done and the results as follows, with changes highlighted in gray:

1. The first step is to identify payments that can be moved and/ or reduced without missing any payments that are due or compromising the financial priorities which you established for yourself.

2. The discretionary items in the budget that could be reduced or moved would seem to be paying yourself (row 20), putting money into your savings account (row 21), deposits to your seed account (row 26), offerings and blessings (row 27), and money for clothes (row 34). You don't want to cut back on or reduce your tithes, because as we learned in earlier chapters, the tithe is the key to God's Financial Plan.

3. Obviously some of the items in #2 above are more important than others, such as savings and your seed account, which you may not want to cut back on initially. Therefore the best way to start is to identify which items if reduced or eliminated would still allow you to stay on track with all or most of your financial priorities. For the purpose of this example, let's assume you decide that while getting some new clothing in April and possibly May when you budget for May, it is not essential. Also remember that when putting the things of God first and trusting Him as your source, there has to be some sacrifice, because if what you decide to go without doesn't cause you some discomfort or doesn't mean anything to you, it won't mean anything to God either!

4. Given that you realize God is your source and understand the importance of giving, let's assume you decide the next items to cut back on are the amount of discretionary money you pay yourself and/or how much you put into a savings account rather than cutting back on what you budgeted for seed, and offerings and money to bless people, at least on this pass of the budget. While you need pocket money and you should save, reducing the amount you pay yourself and/or save will allow you to keep your giving at the level you would like it to be.

5. You next want to see if there are budgeted expenses that can be spread differently with some of the payments pushed out to a future pay period, such as in this example your Property Tax. You owe $750 on May 1, and based on this example your plan was take $600 out of the second April pay period and the remaining $150 out of your May paycheck. You might be able to reduce the April 16 pay period and put more in the May 1 pay period. This is where the total column (Column I) comes in handy as you can see in total how much of the minimum payment you have allocated with the current pay periods for which you are budgeting, and therefore can easily calculate what is left to meet the minimum payment.

6. So you ended up reducing what you pay yourself from $150 to $125 for April 1 and April 16; reduced what you put into your savings account on April 1 and April 16 from $125 to $100; reduced your allocation for a May 1 property tax payment on April 16 from $600 to $400, which means when budgeting for May you need to increase the May 1 Property Tax allocation from $150 to $350; and you eliminated you clothing allowance for April 1 and April 16.

Taking a look at the results and you see the overall shortfall of $745 was reduced to $245, a reduction of $500, with the individual shortfalls for the April 1 and April 16 periods reduced from $210 down to $60 and from $535 down to $185. Great progress, and one more pass should get the budget balanced, as you still have cumulative shortfalls for April 1 and April 16.

The third pass at developing a budget on the next page is our second attempt at trying to balance the budget, with what was done and the results

as follows, with changes highlighted in gray:

1. The budget can be balanced by eliminating deposits to your Savings Account on both April 1 and April 16, and reducing the amount put aside for Offerings/Blessings from $50 to $25 on both April 1 and April 16.

2. While you want to try and put something in a savings account when you can, keeping in mind your financial priorities and the power that God gives you to get wealth, Tithes & Offerings, I believe it says more about where your heart is and whether or not you really trust God as your source if you forego giving to yourself to be able to sow into the Kingdom, those who are a blessing to you, and those you are led to bless, given that you have to choose between giving to yourself (your savings account) or sowing into the Kingdom and those who bless you and who you want to bless (Offerings/Blessings).

3. All cumulative balances are now positive.

As you get close to the time when the last budget period you have budgeted for is coming up, in this case April 16, you need to go through the same process as in this example for the next budgeting periods. When you do, be sure to update all of the balances based on payments made in April, and carry over any surplus you have as the starting balance for the first pay period in the next budgeting cycle, in this example that would be $5. You can do this by placing the surplus in row 41, column D, and creating an

Item	Due Date	Balance	Minimum Payment	April 1st	April 16th	Total
1. Tithe	as paid	n/a	10% gross pay	$300	$300	$600
2. Telephone	16th	n/a	$100	$0	$100	$100
3. Mortgage	10th	$50,000	$500	$500	$0	$500
4. Credit Cards	10th	$2,000	$200	$200	$0	$200
5. Car Payment	15th	$7,500	$350	$0	$350	$350
6. Groceries	weekly	n/a	$150	$150	$150	$300
7. Insurances	1st	$5,400	$900	$650	$250	$900
8. Gas/Electric	25th	n/a	$200	$0	$200	$200
9. Cable TV	16th	n/a	$150	$0	$150	$150
10. Self	as paid	n/a	$150	$125	$125	$250
11. Savings	monthly	n/a	$250	$0	$0	$0
12. Property Tax	1st day of 2nd month of qtr.	$3,000	$750	$0	$400	$400
13. Subscriptions	annual	$200	$120	$10	$10	$20
14. Seed	as paid		$25	$25	$25	$50
15. Offerings/Blessings	as paid	n/a	$50	$25	$25	$50
16. Gasoline	weekly	n/a	$50	$50	$50	$100
17. Clothes	as needed	$2,500/year	$200	$0	$0	$0
18. Internet	21st	n/a	$25	$0	$25	$25
Total				$2,035	$2,160	$4,195
Net Pay				$2,100	$2,100	$4,200
Balance				$65	($60)	$5
Cumulative Balance				$65	$5	
Gross Pay				$3,000	$3,000	$6,000

Excel formula in row 42, column E reflecting the cumulative balance of the carryover surplus from April 16 plus any surplus or shortfall for May 1.

This was a simple example of how you set up a budget for yourself. The additional passes or versions of the budget you may have to go through will not always be as easy as they were here. In some cases you may have to eliminate paying more than one item all together, starting with discretionary items. You may find, depending upon your financial situation, that you may not be able to make all of the minimum payments on non-discretionary bills you have. In those cases it may be wise to contact those accounts you will not be able to pay in a particular billing period, either in full or in part, and let them know your payment will be late, and/or work out a payment plan that fits your budget until you are current. Also, as mentioned previously, consider the use of wise counsel if you find that you can use some help developing your budget. And whatever you do to balance your budget, keep trusting God as your source while you follow your financial priorities.

Now let's talk a little bit about savings accounts. On the next page is the savings account template I use, which is set up much the same way as the basic budget/checking account template above with Excel doing the math, across and down. I use only one savings account so as to generate as much bank interest as I can, and use the spreadsheet to keep track of what the money in my savings account is allocated for and to budget what I plan to deposit and withdraw from it each pay period.

The items for which I have put money in my savings account are in the first column, with the dates corresponding to the dates in the budget/checking account example used above for April going across the top row.

Here is how this template works:

Item	4/1	4/1	4/1	4/16	4/16
Savings	$500	$0	$500	$0	$500
Seed	$200	$25	$225	$25	$250
Property Tax	$0	$350	$350	$400	$750
Offerings and Blessings	$150	$25	$175	$25	$200
Clothes	$500	($350)	$150	$0	$150
	$1,350	$50	$1,400	$450	$1,850

1. The first 4/1 entry lists the money in the account on the starting date, in this example April 1, and the breakdown by category, which is the same categories used in the budget/checking account example.

2. The "Savings" entry, for example, represents money I set aside strictly to save.

3. The second 4/1 entry lists deposits and withdrawals for the 4/1 pay period, all but one are based on the budgeted allocations for 4/1 in the budget/checking account example above - $25 from Checking to the Savings for the Seed Account, and $25 from Checking to Savings set aside for Offerings/Blessings.

4. The one exception is the ($350) withdrawal from the Clothes allocation that is not being withdrawn, but re-directed to the Property Tax allocation. If you recall, the original checking budget had $600 allocated for property taxes on April 16, which was to be put aside for the May 1 quarterly property tax payment of $750 with the remaining $150 to be taken from the May 1 pay period. To balance the budget the Property Tax allocation on April 16 was reduced to $400 meaning $350 would

now have to be taken from the May 1 pay period to meet the $750 May 1 Property Tax payment. Since there is $500 already in the Savings account allocated for Clothes, a wise decision would be to reallocate $350 from the Clothes allocation to the Property Tax allocation, which along with the $400 coming out of the April 16 pay period for Property Tax makes up the $750 needed for the May 1 Property Tax payment. In this way nothing has to be allocated out of the May 1 pay period for Property Tax, leaving the money that was going to be allocated from the May 1 pay period for Property Tax ($350) for other bills and/or making up for some of the items that had to be cut or eliminated for the two April pay periods in order to balance the budget.

5. The Excel spreadsheet calculates the budgeted deposits and withdrawals planned for 4/1, displaying the "net" of the deposits and withdrawals at the bottom, which is $50. This tells me that on 4/1 I want to transfer $50 from my checking account to my savings account.

6. The third and final 4/1 entry sums the first two 4/1 entries across and down, to let me know after the $50 transfer from the checking account to the savings account, what the total balance is in the savings account, $1,400, and the balance for each individual item.

7. The first 4/16 entry indicates what the budgeted deposits and withdrawals are planned for 4/16, with the $450 at the bottom telling me that on 4/16 I should transfer $450 from the checking account into the savings account.

8. The second 4/16 entry gives a total savings account balance and balances each item after the 4/16 transfer has been made.

When you plan for the next two-month budget period or for however many months you plan to budget, the three 4/1 entries would be replaced with 5/1 entries, with the starting balances as of 5/1 under the first 5/1 entry being the balances you had as of 4/16. I know this may be confusing, but once you do it, it will make a lot more sense – so don't be discouraged. And keep in mind that you don't have to use a computer. You can do this by hand; just make sure you have a good eraser on your pencil!

Since the savings account is based on the final balanced budget/checking account, you should balance the budget/checking account template first, before setting up or updating your savings account template. Once you've got the budget or budget checking account balanced, setting up the initial savings account and updating it going forward is really quite easy.

I know this was only one simple (or maybe not-so-simple) example of the kinds of challenges you will face as you develop and balance your budget, but as you work with the budget more and more and go through several iterations of your budget, it will become easier for you. For now, it's important that you understand the concept of budgeting and one way to go about it. Remember, this isn't the only way to develop a budget, but just one of many but one I know works well from having used it over the years. Also remember that developing the budget is not the end game, just one aspect of being an effective steward over the financial blessings with which God entrusts you.

Now that you've got the budgeting process under your belt, let's move on the Stewardship 104 in the next chapter. But before we do, here are a few scriptures and questions to review and answer:

1. **1 Corinthians 9:26-27:** What do these verses say about discipline? What can happen if you do not discipline yourself?

2. **Romans 12:1:** What are you to do with you body, and why? What does "your reasonable service" mean to you?

3. **Hebrews 12:2-4 & Luke 22:41-43:** What do these passages tell you about Jesus? How did Jesus discipline Himself?

4. **Hebrews 11:1:** According to this verse what is faith? How would you define faith in your words after reading this verse?

5. **Mark 11:24:** What does this verse say that you should do when you pray? What does this verse say will happen if you obey it?

6. **Romans 12:2:** What does Paul say you are to do with your thinking, and how do you think you are to do that?

7. **Joshua 1:8:** This short verse says that if you do this one thing, you will be prosperous and have good success. What is this one thing, and how do you do it?

Chapter 9

The Way to Keep on Track

So far, you've learned what being a steward is all about, what and how to establish Financial Priorities, and how to develop and balance your budget. Now what? You've got a budget and you need to stick to it. This requires self-discipline and faith, especially when starting from a position of financial bondage or inexperience. The enemy will do all he can to discourage you, try and make you think your budget won't work or is unrealistic. He'll tempt you to believe that you deserve to splurge, to go buy things you want, but don't really need. He will use anything to defeat and keep you in financial bondage. When he does all that, you need to fight back!

If you try to do that based on your own will and ability, however, the enemy will defeat you. It will take a combination of your own will, self-discipline, and faith to win this battle. In this chapter we will discuss self-discipline and faith, key components to becoming an effective steward over the financial resources God entrusts to you. We will see how these three practices work to refute the deceptions of the enemy and to help you stick with your budget, be an effective steward, attain Kingdom Prosperity, and "have more than enough."

To understand self-discipline you need first to understand the concept of discipline, which is not punishment, but rather an orderly or prescribed pattern of behavior that shows a willingness to obey rules and orders. Your budget is a set of rules or a prescribed pattern of behavior. If you have understood the principles of Kingdom Prosperity and Effective Financial Stewardship up to this point, you have developed a budget that is based on sound biblical principles that are consistent with God's Financial Plan and that incorporates the proper Financial Priorities.

Self-discipline is the application of discipline where your budget is concerned so that you can willingly follow or obey the rules and order dictated by your budget with an attitude of appreciation and respect for the financial resources God has entrusted to you. Self-discipline can also be thought of as the ability to make yourself do things that should be done, like stick to your budget, exercising restraint over your impulse to stray from your budget and satisfy the desire to spend your money on whatever satisfies you or gives you instant gratification. Self-discipline is making yourself follow the rules or prescribed pattern of spending behavior defined by your budget.

Self-discipline or disciplining yourself is biblical. I Corinthians 9:26-27 states, "*Therefore I run thus: not with uncertainty. Thus I fight: not as one who beats the air. But I discipline my body and bring it into subjection, lest, when I have preached to others, I myself should become disqualified.*" Disciplining your body is a form of self-discipline as you subject your body to the rules or prescribed pattern of behavior that you have set forth as a result of choosing to obey Romans 12:1: "*I beseech you therefore, brethren, by the mercies of God, that you present your bodies a living sacrifice, holy, acceptable to God, which is your reasonable service.*"

In terms of being an effective Steward over your financial resources, self-discipline is the process of bringing your whole being (spirit, soul and body) under submission to the rules and prescribed pattern of behavior dictated by your budget. Hebrews 12:2-4 describes the self-discipline that Jesus had:

"Looking unto Jesus, the author and finisher of our faith, who for the joy that was set before Him endured the cross, despising the shame, and has sat down at the right hand of the throne of God. For consider Him who endured such hostility from sinners against Himself, lest you become weary and discouraged in your souls. You have not yet resisted to bloodshed, striving against sin."

Jesus didn't have to go to the cross for us, but he endured the cross, disciplining himself to pay the price that we could never pay to be reconciled to God. We also see Jesus' self-discipline portrayed in Luke 22:41-43:

"And He was withdrawn from them about a stone's throw, and He knelt down and prayed, saying, "Father, if it is Your will, take this cup away from Me; nevertheless not My will, but Yours, be done. " Then an angel appeared to Him from heaven, strengthening Him."

If Jesus exercised self-discipline to take a brutal beating and die for you and me, how little is it for us to yield to the will of God and follow our budget so we manage the financial resources God has given us? I would say not very much at all!

Notice something else from Luke. Jesus said, *"Nevertheless not My will, but Yours, be done."* You see there that Jesus had a choice to make, and that was to follow God's will or his will. He chose to follow God's will. The point is that self-discipline requires a conscious decision to follow the rules or a predetermined pattern of behavior. This is often not an easy thing to do, but when we do so, God will work with us and give us the strength to stick with His will and not ours, as we see in verse 43 where it says *"Then an angel appeared to Him from heaven, strengthening Him."* If you are going to follow your budget no matter what your circumstances may look like and despite the deceptions of the enemy, you have to first make a conscious decision to self-discipline yourself, and with the help of the Lord be strong enough to follow through on that decision.

Self-discipline alone, however, is not enough. Jesus was able to follow through on his decision to self-discipline Himself, submit to God's will and endure the cross on our behalf because he believed His Father would bring Him through that ordeal and breathe life back into Him. In other words, Jesus had faith in God. We too, if we are to follow our budget, we also need to exercise faith along with self-disciplining ourselves to follow our budget. When we talk about faith, we're talking about trusting God to do what He said he would do, to meet all of our needs if we would seek Him first and His righteousness (see Matthew 6:33).

The Bible defines faith in Hebrews 11:1: *"Now faith is the substance of things hoped for, the evidence of things not seen."* This tells us that faith is first of all present tense, (*Now faith is*), not past or future. It also tells us that faith is the reality (*substance*) of the future good we are expecting (*things hoped for*), and the proof (*evidence*) that the future good we are expecting (*things not seen*) already exists. Where there is hope substantiated by proof, there is confidence that the future good we are expecting will come to pass. That's why Jesus told us in Mark 11:24: "*Therefore I say to you, whatever things you ask when you pray, believe that you receive them, and you will have them.*" Therefore exercising our faith along with self-discipline to follow your budget is:

1. Making a conscious decision to follow a budget;

2. Knowing what the Word of God says about where God sees you financially;

3. Asking for the financial breakthrough you need based on His Word;

4. Believing you receive that breakthrough when you ask Him for it;

5. Confessing that you have that breakthrough; and

6. Acting on belief and confession by following your budget.

Those six steps comprise good stewardship, and spell out how you can realize Kingdom Prosperity in your life.

No one gets into financial bondage overnight, and therefore no one gets out of it overnight. Some people have been in financial bondage for the better part of their adult lives. Getting out of that financial bondage will be a process. If you follow the biblical principles of Kingdom Prosperity and Successful Financial Stewardship outlined in this book, you will be delivered from financial bondage and enjoy financial prosperity in less time than it took to get into financial bondage.

There is also another component to become an effective financial steward and that is sacrifice. *Financial Prosperity and responsible fiscal management (effective stewardship) will sometimes require personal sacrifice, but will always require self-discipline and faith."* We've talked about self-discipline and faith, so let's spend a little time talking about sacrifice. One definition of sacrifice is *"the act of giving up something that you want to keep especially in order to get or do something else or to help someone."* If you are going to follow your budget, some sacrifice will be necessary.

Part of self-discipline is learning to say "No" to the things you want, and to say yes to what God wants you to do. As it relates to Kingdom Prosperity, that means there will be times when you will have to go without some things you want but don't really need to stick to your budget. This is where self-discipline comes in, because it will take self-discipline in order to sacrifice. It may mean not taking a vacation for a year or so, not being able to give everyone what they want for Christmas, not buying a new car right now, not dining out as much, or not buying new clothes for a period of time.

While sacrifice is always painful when you are going through it, you will be glad you did so when you achieve the financial breakthrough you have been seeking for such a long time. There is no magic formula for when and or how long to make financial sacrifices, but the key is to be guided by your financial priorities, budget and faith in the financial breakthrough for which you are believing God. Here are a few guidelines I have used over the years to determine what financial sacrifices I need to make. The list is not exhaustive and I am sure there are some effective guidelines I am missing. These are the ones that have worked for me:

1. Don't spend what you don't have;

2. Purchase only what you need, not what you want;

3. Don't be concerned about keeping up with the Jones's;

4. Learn how to go without;

5. Always trust God as your source, instead of yourself or any other person or thing in this world; and

6. Keep the "pay me now or pay me later" principle in proper perspective: Everything costs something sooner or

later, so don't be fooled by deceptions like "no interest for the first year," "no payments for 18 months," or "low monthly payment terms available" – just to name a few.

I recently read an article by Danielle Braff in the *Chicago Tribune,* which I found helpful as a guide to spending any discretionary or extra money you may have. Just because you have a few extra dollars isn't a license to go spend it all. The article talks about the common shopping dilemma of buying what you love now, which might be trendier and more expensive, verses what you think you'll love in 10 years, which might have a higher re-sale value and be a classic even though it might not have that just-gotta-have-it allure at first sight. The article quotes several authors concerning shopping guidelines.

Mark Ellwood, author of *Bargain Fever: How to Shop in a Discounted World*, has a clear shopping formula for buying trendy items verses staples. Ellwood suggests that you classify your purchases into three categories: investments, durable or trendy. His advice is not ever spending more than $50 for anything in the trendy category.[3] Melissa Tosetti, author of *Living the Savvy Life: The Savvy Woman's Guide to Smart Spending and Rich Living*, said that you can be more flexible depending on your financial status, but the overall message is the same as Ellwood - be purposeful when you shop.[4]

Tosetti says that if you've fallen in love with a trendy item, then get it, even if you're only going to love it for a year or so. "But if it's something that two weeks later, you're not going to think about again, you shouldn't buy it." **The key is to** determine which items you're only going to love for two weeks, and which are the keepers for a longer period of time. Look around at the clutter in your house, and see if any of it was purchased just a few weeks ago because you felt you just had to have it. "Unless you really think about it, you're just going to keep doing what you're doing," You should invest well in items that you plan on using on a regular basis, such as kitchen knives, pots and pans and wardrobe classics. Unless you're a professional cook, however, there's no reason to buy the very best knives on the market. "You want the best of what you're going to use them for," Tosetti said. "Make individual decisions instead of blanket decisions."[5]

Kelly Hancock, author of *Saving Savvy*, warns that buying an expensive classic item in the hopes you can resell it later doesn't always work. "I find resale value plummets very quickly and much lower than you would imagine," she said. If you do plan on buying and reselling keep in mind that "Classic items will hold their value over time, and on-trend, more premium items generally retain strong resale value within a few-year period," said James Reinhart, CEO and co-founder of thredUP.com, an online clothing consignment store. "The time to really think about resale value and contemplate whether you're buying a classic item that you'll keep forever … is when the price tag is higher than what you would normally spend," he added.[6] While none of these guidelines are the end-all, cure-all, they might be helpful with regard to self-disciplining yourself and making some sacrifices mixed with your faith in order to live within your budget.

One last thing that needs to be understood so you can stay on track with your budget, and that's the way you think. If you either haven't managed your finances very well or not as effectively as you could have, in order to apply the principles of Kingdom Prosperity including developing and sticking to your budget, it's going to require that you change the way you define prosperity, what money is really for and what being in debt really means. I know I covered these topics in the first three chapters of this book, but the way you think about prosperity, money and debt will have a direct impact on your ability to exercise your faith and self-discipline in trying to stick to your budget.

Romans 12:1-2 from *The Message Bible* says:

"So here's what I want you to do, God helping you: Take your everyday, ordinary life—your sleeping, eating, going-to-work, and walking-around life—and place it before God as an offering. Embracing what God does for you is the best thing you can do for

him. Don't become so well-adjusted to your culture that you fit into it without even thinking. Instead, fix your attention on God. You'll be changed from the inside out. Readily recognize what he wants from you, and quickly respond to it. Unlike the culture around you, always dragging you down to its level of immaturity, God brings the best out of you, develops well-formed maturity in you" (emphasis added).

Focus on verse 2 that reads from the New King James version of the Bible as follows: *"And do not be conformed to this world, but be transformed by the renewing of your mind, that you may prove what is that good and acceptable and perfect will of God."* If you want godly results in your finances or in any area of your life, you need to think like God and also speak like God. God thinking comes from identifying all of the garbage with which the world has brainwashed you over the years and replacing it with what God says from His Word.

Once you know what God thinks, then you should speak that over and over into your life. The more you think and speak what God thinks and speaks, slowly but surely you will begin to move or act on what you believe in your heart and confess with your mouth. You will only know what God thinks and come to believe it in your heart if you spend time with Him and His Word, meditating on it continually and settling in your heart that it is true. Then, as Joshua 1:8 predicts, you will become prosperous and have good success: *"This book of the Law shall not depart from your mouth, but you shall meditate in it day and night, that you may observe to do according to all that is written in it. For then you will make your way prosperous, and then you will have good success."* This is how you transition your mind to God's way of thinking and get to the point where you exercise your faith and self-discipline.

So in these last four chapters, we've learned about successful financial stewardship. In the next chapter we'll cover a few other practical principles to help you be an effective steward and achieve the kind of Kingdom prosperity in your life God wants you to have.

Here are just two verses and one question before moving on to the next chapter.

Genesis 2:24; Ephesians 5:31 - What do these two verses of scripture say to you personally about how a husband and wife are to live their lives?

Part 4

The Conclusion

Mixing common sense with biblical wisdom.

Chapter 10

Practical Principles for Kingdom Prosperity

I want to share a few more ideas for achieving Kingdom Prosperity in life and being an effective Financial Steward, primarily as it relates to the family unit, and in particular husbands and wives. My late wife and I were not aware of and did not apply most of these ideas in our early marriage years. Once we did in conjunction with other biblical and practical principles shared in this book, we began to get our financial matters in order and grow in Kingdom Prosperity. I sub-titled this chapter "Mixing Common Sense with Biblical Wisdom" because, while these ideas have a biblical basis, it takes revelation and common sense to apply and get the most out of them.

There are any number of additional passages that provide the biblical basis for these ideas as it relates to financial matters between the husband and the wife, but I want to refer to just two here that I believe are an umbrella for all of the others. This biblical strength for marriage comes from Genesis 2:24 (emphasis added): *"Therefore a man shall leave his father and mother and be joined to his wife, and they shall become one flesh"*, and Ephesians 5:31 (emphasis added): *"For this reason a man shall leave his father and mother and be joined to his wife, and the two shall become one flesh"*.

When many couples get married they do not fully comprehend what becoming one flesh with one another truly means. Simply stated, it means the husband and wife are to function as one. Most newlyweds and even some couples who have been married for a while apply this in some areas of their lives, but each generally still have some things that they hold on to individually. I am not saying a man and wife should not each have their own space or time for themselves without their spouse, but there are certain areas most couples tend to overlook when it comes to living as "one flesh." I am not a marriage expert even though I was married for a long time, so I am not going to attempt to fully describe this concept of being one flesh. I do know after many years of marriage, however, that one of the most important and rewarding areas is being one flesh in the area of money.

The first concept that I deem important for the one flesh truth is that *"all financial assets and debts in a marriage belong to the husband and wife regardless of who was responsible for bringing those assets and debts into the household or marriage".* If husband and wife are truly one flesh then they own everything of any material value together, like their home, automobile(s), and other assets. The same should hold true of any investments and major purchases made during the marriage. In addition, as one flesh the debts that the husband and wife each bring into the marriage belong to both. It may be that the agreement on how certain debts are to be paid down or paid off may be that one spouse or the other will handle that debt, but the debts belong to both spouses. In the case of a home, which is the most significant investment a husband and wife (or an individual for that matter) ever makes, as one flesh the deed should be in the name of both the husband and the wife, even in those situations where one spouse or the other owned the home before getting married and brought the home into the marriage.

Not to collectively own all assets and debts in a marriage says that one is not fully joined to their spouse as one flesh. The verses in Genesis and Ephesians on the previous page say that the man and woman "become *one flesh.*" If husband and wife are truly one, why wouldn't they share everything of any consequence? If husband and wife are not joint owners of their combined assets and debts, it seems to insinuate that one or the other, or both, do not fully trust the other. Without complete trust between a husband and wife, it probably won't be long before the marriage is in trouble.

Going along with the first concept is the second that *"all financial decisions in the household are made together, with husband and wife coming into agreement."* What does it say about the trust between a husband and wife if one spouse makes a decision about a major financial purchase or investment without consulting their spouse, and then goes ahead and carries out that decision on their own? I'm not talking about when one spouse goes out and makes purchases with money that both parties agreed was under that partner's control. What I am talking are things like the budget, putting money aside for the children's college education, money for a vacation fund, and loaning money to someone, especially relatives. In all those cases, the husband and wife need to be in total agreement. Not only does not making these types of financial decisions independent of one another show distrust, it also usually ends up as a source of division and strife between husband and wife. That does nothing to strengthen the marriage but instead weakens or deteriorates the closeness and intimacy between husband and wife.

My third cardinal rule for a couple's financial health is: *"husband and wife should review their financial situation before getting married (assets, liabilities, accounts, etc.), and decide how they will manage their finances before entering into the marriage.*" This practice will avoid many of the pitfalls discussed under ideas one and two above. Most couples don't have that prenuptial meeting. We get so wrapped up in each other that managing the family finances is never discussed until it becomes a problem in the marriage. The good news is that even if you and your spouse did not discuss how you would manage your finances before you got married, take the opportunity to have the discussion on how you want to manage family finances after you have taken your vows. It's not too late. That discussion cannot be a five- or ten-minute discussion, or in fact not a one-hour or one-session discussion. It will probably take place over the course of several weeks, especially when areas of managing the family finances come up that husband and wife do not agree upon, which will happen. This takes time to talk and pray through so that an agreement can be reached.

Idea four supports idea three: "*Consider the use of a financial professional.*" This can take on several different scenarios. You may want to use a professional to help walk through and reach agreement on what your financial priorities are as discussed in an earlier chapter, to help you determine how to move forward in areas where you do agree, or to plan your investment polio. You can talk with family members about this, but if you do as I cautioned in an earlier chapter, you will need to be comfortable sharing confidential information with your family. My late wife and I talked with family members not to resolve any specific differences we had about managing our finances, but to get advice as to how to go about resolving them, getting input more about the process than any specific issue.

Idea five is that *"there should be only joint accounts in a marriage as it relates to financial matters"*. I've seen this become a source of strife in many marriages where one spouse or the other has a separate account or "stash" just for himself or herself. Now the husband and wife may agree that each can have an account of their own for money from various sources – investments, inheritance, earnings and the like. When the husband or wife opens a separate account without having discussed and come into agreement with their partner as to why they want a separate account, however, the spirit of distrust will surely rear its ugly head up and create a rift or division between husband and wife. There are any number of areas which if not "covered" can provide an opening for the enemy to slip into the marriage and try to raise havoc. Lack of trust or even the appearance of the lack of trust on the part of one spouse or the other is probably the one area where the enemy has caused the most problems in a marriage, especially as it relates to money.

Think about it. What does it say to the husband or wife about the other spouse if one day they inadvertently find out the other spouse has been keeping a separate financial account without the knowledge and agreement of the other spouse? Doesn't he or she trust me? What's this all about? Has my husband or wife been hiding some of their income from me? Is he or she having an affair? And the questions this type of situation can raise goes on and on. Then there is the question of how to broach this type of issue with your spouse? When and how should I confront them? What will their reaction be? Should I even say anything? Maybe I should just go open my own separate private account? Having planted the seeds of doubt and distrust the enemy will stop at nothing to rip the husband and wife apart, because he comes to steal, kill and destroy.

Number six has to do with *"setting your pride aside or checking your ego at the door."* In any partnership there are going to be things that one partner is better at than the other and that usually works both ways. One partner should not have the attitude that he or she is better at everything than the other partner. Otherwise, the partnership is doomed. Just as this is true in business or professional partnerships, so it is true in the marriage. As this idea relates to finances it means that husband and wife need to find out who is better and can do the best job for the them as a couple with each aspect of managing the household finances. Let whoever does what they do best, do that as often as possible.

For example, when my late wife and I talked about who would do what as far as handling our finances, two of the tasks we agreed I would handle were developing the budget and paying the bills. My wife was good at those things as well. I really enjoyed working with numbers, however, and had a little more experience that she did with spreadsheets, I also had the patience and discipline to sit down twice a month and pay all of the bills.

Now this didn't mean I developed the budget and paid the bills without her input because we were a partnership or team. I would consult my wife about certain items impacting the budget and we would reach agreement as to how we wanted to handle those things. I would then use that information in "drafting" the budget. Once the draft was done, my wife and I would review it and discuss any items either of us had any questions about, which would usually result in some revisions to the budget.

Once I finalized the budget, we would each have our own copy to follow. I would pay bills when they came in according to the budget we had agreed upon, again, consulting with my wife on adjustments we needed to make to the budget if a bill might have exceeded what we estimated or if the bills overall were less and we had money left over at the end of the month. We followed this process each month and it worked quite well. Conversely, my wife would do all of the negotiating with creditors when necessary, not just or only when we couldn't meet all of our obligations, but also and for the most part when we were looking for better payment terms. We were both very good negotiators, but she had more patience than I did and a much better disposition for this type of negotiation than I. Again, the point is to let whoever does what they do best, do that as often as possible.

The last couple of ideas have to do with understanding that a marriage is a three-way partnership between the husband, wife and Christ. Therefore, idea seven is to "*be flexible*." Depending on your age when you get married and how long you have been living on your own with no one to answer to except yourself, the degree of difficulty in learning to be flexible and compromise will vary from somewhat easy to very hard. No matter what the degree of difficulty, however, it will be absolutely essential to be flexible. Both husband and wife need to be willing to "give and take" as it were, and to adjust, make changes, do some things differently, and give up some control.

While this idea applies to most if not all areas of a marriage, it definitely applies to how the husband and wife will handle their finances. It's been said that the three biggest areas that cause problems in a marriage are communication, sex and money. And if husband and/or wife are not flexible in their communication with each other and in seeking the wisdom of the

Lord about how they will handle their money or manage their finances, then they open a door or give place for the enemy to come in and cause division and conflict between husband and wife. Not only will their relationship be strained, but they will most likely not handle their money the way God wants them to, not be effective financial stewards, and definitely not be walking as one flesh in this area of their life.

This concept of flexibility applies not only to the individual views of the husband and wife, but also with respect to what the Lord is saying to the husband and wife collectively. The husband and wife may be in agreement as to how to handle a certain aspect of the finances, but the Lord sees it differently. Therefore the husband and wife have to be flexible enough even when they are in agreement to yield to the leading of the Lord.

Going right along with flexibility are the ideas of *"being open and honest with each other."* If husbands and wives are to come into agreement regarding their finances, they can have no secrets. Everything must be out in the open with nothing held back. After all, the husband and wife are now one flesh. What one or the other might try to hold back or not be totally honest about will eventually come back to bite both the husband and wife regardless of which one is not being honest or trying to not share something. When it does, the fallout will be worse than if the husband or wife had shared that aspect of their financial decisions up front. You may be ashamed of something you did in your past regarding how you handled and managed your financial resources, but if you can't share that with your wife, who else in the world can you share it with?

The last two ideas involve "*being patient and humble,*" especially early on in a marriage after the husband and wife have come into agreement on how to handle and manage their finances. It's all too easy for one spouse or the other to sit back after both spouses have agreed on a course of action and privately criticize the other spouse if things don't go the way the spouse who has given up control over that aspect of the finances doesn't like the way things are going. They may start thinking "I could have handled that better," "that's not the way I would have done it," or "Look how long it takes he or she to get that done." If you let this kind of murmuring go on unchecked, it will eventually boil over one day and could lead to a blow up between your husband or wife. You need to remember who you are and whose you are. God gives grace to the humble but resists the proud (see James 4:6 and I Peter 5:5). Rather, pull those thoughts down, take them into captivity, cast them down and punish them according to 2 Corinthians 10:4-6.

One way to avoid getting caught up in pride and impatience as it relates to finances in the marriage is to agree up front once you have settled how to handle your finances that it's okay for one to ask the other from time to time how they are doing with whatever aspects of the couple's finances each is responsible for. Also agree up front that if one spouse or another is having difficulty with what they are responsible for, it's permissible to ask for help, and if one spouse or the other is troubled by the way the other is handling something that it's okay to bring that up.

I remember that after a few years of marriage my wife approached me and said she'd like to handle the paying of the bills for a while. I agreed because I knew she could do it, and also because it would give me a break. After about three or four months, she asked me if I wanted to take over paying the bills again. Rather than let my ego or pride rise up and say something stupid like "Oh, are you having trouble?" or "Is it too hard for you?", I just said that if she was sure she wanted me to do that again I would. There were no arguments, no criticism. A month or so later she thanked me for agreeing to pay the bills again without asking her why she no longer wanted to do it.

This list is not meant to be all inclusive and I'm sure there are many more ideas that are helpful for husband and wife to consider in managing their finances, but these are just a few I have found most helpful over the years which I believe all husbands and wives can benefit from.

So what are you going to do now?

Chapter 11

The Challenge

By now I trust you have a better understanding of Kingdom Prosperity and God's Plan for Successful Financial Stewardship. The question at this point is: What will you do with it? You could simply say that was a nice book and put it in your library to collect dust, never to see the light of day again. You could try and follow some of the principles and concepts we've learned, until you reach a point where it starts to get too hard to apply them to your own situation and then put the book down and never look at it again. You might even decide you don't agree what I've shared in this book, that you're doing just fine and don't need any of this stuff, or that you don't have the time. You may just not want to change your present situation. If you decide to go down any of these roads, that's your choice and I wish you the best.

How about something a little more radical? How about actually deciding that no matter what your present financial condition is, it can be better, and that you will try to do it God's way. Even if you are already managing your finances God's way, as it is with anything in the Kingdom of God, there is always room for improvement and growth. Don't let the enemy steal the blessings God wants you to have. Don't give him "place" in your life by deciding you're doing just fine on your own, or by copping an attitude that you've been doing it God's way and there isn't anything else you need to know or learn.

James 4:7 instructs you first to submit to God, then resist the devil and he will flee from you. Even if you decide that what I've shared in this book is not for you, I pray that it has inspired you enough to seek the Lord on your own about your present financial condition and submit to what His financial plan for you. If you find some better ways to be an effective financial steward and realize Kingdom Prosperity in your life, let me know so I can get in on it too. If you've learned anything from this book, however, take whatever that is and faithfully apply it according to the biblical principles that have been shared, and be, do and have all that God wants you to have.

Well, I've taken up enough your time and I want to thank you for giving up a part of your life to read what the Lord gave me to share with you. I truly believe it is no accident that you picked up this book and read it. Since you've invested some of your time already, why not invest a little more and apply what you've learned in your own financial situation?

Until next time, be blessed!

Endnotes

[1] C. Peter Wagner, *Discover Your Spiritual Gifts* (Regal Publishers: Scottsdale, Arizona), page 55.

[2] Definition for 'steward', accessed March 17, 2015 from www. merriam-webster.com.

[3] Danielle Braff. *Chicago Tribune* (April 24, 2014).

[4] Danielle Braff. *Chicago Tribune* (April 24, 2014).

[5] Danielle Braff. *Chicago Tribune* (April 24, 2014).

[6] Danielle Braff. *Chicago Tribune* (April 24, 2014).